A FIREFLY GARDENER'S GUIDE

THE TOMATO HANDBOOK

JENNIFER BENNETT

FIREFLY BOOKS

A FIREFLY BOOK

Cataloguing-in-Publication Data

Bennett, Jennifer
    The tomato handbook : tips & tricks for growing the best tomatoes

(A Firefly gardener's guide)
Includes index.
ISBN 1-55209 107 4

1. Tomatoes.   I. Title.   II. Series.

SB349.B46 1997   635'.642   C97-930036 3

Published by
Firefly Books Ltd.
3680 Victoria Park Avenue
Willowdale, Ontario
Canada M2H 3K1

Published in the U.S. by
Firefly Books (U.S.) Inc.
P.O. Box 1338, Ellicott Station
Buffalo, New York 14205

Produced by
Bookmakers Press Inc.
12 Pine Street
Kingston, Ontario K7K 1W1

Design by
Linda J. Menyes
Q Kumquat Designs

Color separations by
Friesens
Altona, Manitoba

Printed and bound in Canada by
Friesens
Altona, Manitoba

Printed on acid-free paper

Front cover photograph by Turid Forsyth

Back cover photograph by Turid Forsyth

Acknowledgments

The Tomato Handbook, in its finished state, represents the commitment and cooperation of several individuals. They include Linda Menyes, Q Kumquat Designs; copy editor Charlotte DuChene and editorial associates Catherine DeLury and Mary Patton; principal photographers Turid Forsyth and Walter Chandoha; and Susan Dickinson and Tracy Read of Bookmakers Press.

Contents

Introducing the Tomato

From Wolf Peach to Big Boy

The story of the tomato is a tale of three continents: South America, Europe and North America, in that order. The story ends here and now, with the tomato standing in the proud and somewhat surprising position of most popular vegetable in North America, the lush centerfold of the garden at the turn of the millennium. The previous part of the story, the European chapter, began in the 1500s, when Spanish and Portuguese explorers looted from Central and South America not only artistic and cultural treasures but also some unusual vegetables, one of which was a round red, yellow or orange fruit the native Nahua people called *tomatl*.

Even then, the tomato bore scant resemblance to its ancestors growing on the slopes of the Andes. The wild grandparents of cultivated tomatoes were tender perennials with marble-sized, sometimes fuzzy berries and foliage smelly enough to keep most predators away. But by the time Europeans arrived, bigger and more luscious fruit had been selected for so long that the markets and gardens of South and Central America already featured the *tomatl* in a dazzling array of sizes of roundish shapes and sunny colors, much like today's salad tomatoes, paste tomatoes and cherry tomatoes.

When they were taken back to Europe, the new vegetables lost their glamour. The tomato was called "wolf peach," origin of the Latin genus name *Lycopersicon*, because of its evident membership in the plant family Solanaceae, the nightshades. This was "a suspicious family," according to the Swedish botanist Linnaeus. Among the solanaceous plants Europeans knew well was another wolf plant, monkshood, sometimes called wolfsbane because it was poisonous enough to kill the most vicious predator the people knew. Also related to the immigrant *tomatl* were henbane, datura, mandrake and nightshade itself, all plants that could be used medicinally with care but were better known as hallucinogens and poisons. You might as well cook a mandrake pie as make sauce from tomatoes, sometimes dubbed *mala insana*, the "unwholesome fruit."

"We only have them for curiosity in our Gardens, and for the amorous aspect or beauty of the fruit," wrote Englishman John Parkinson in his herbal of 1629. He described three types: "Great Apple of Love the ordinary red sort," "Yellow Amorous Apples" and "Small Love Apples." To this day, the tomato bears the signature of its contrary nature and mixed press, *Lycopersicon esculentum*—which can be roughly translated as "wolf peach edible."

The "edible" reassurance, *esculentum*, came first from Italy, where, for some reason, the local cuisine embraced the newcomer—maybe pizza recognized its soul mate on sight. There, the yellow-fruited type was called golden apple, *pomo d'òro*, a name that altered only a little, perhaps, to become *pomo amoris*, love apple. On the other hand, that fond moniker—turned into "amorous apple" and "great apple of love" by John Parkinson—may have arisen from the tomato's reputation as an aphrodisiac, a fate that befell many a round, red, juicy, sensual-looking fruit during an era when vegetables were linked to human health by their appearance.

TOMATOES IN NORTH AMERICA

Love apples made the return journey across the Atlantic with settlers from Europe and, on the report of Thomas Jefferson, were grown in gardens in the state of Virginia by the 1780s. Still, suspicion lingered until, according to legend, Robert Gibbon Johnson ate a ripe one on the steps of the courthouse of Salem, New Jersey, in 1820, in full and foolhardy view of all. The courageous fellow survived, and the tomato went on to become a rising starlet in the otherwise rather bland history of vegetables. Ohio cornered the new sensation as its state fruit. By the 1870s, canned tomatoes were becoming popular as off-season replacements for summer's fresh harvest. Thus was the Joseph Campbell Company born, and tomato soup became almost as American as apple pie. Since 1920, per capita tomato consumption in the United States has tripled, thanks in large part to the tomato's eminent suitability for sauces and condiments. This adaptable vegetable is the sauce of the fast-food in-

In North America, the tomato is a starlet, compared with other vegetables.

dustry, the smile on the face of the Campbell kid.

There are some 3,000 varieties of tomato today, an ever-rising number that reflects the plant's amenability to being bred. Different shapes, colors and sizes already existed when the fruit was discovered by Europeans, but the beef-steak, with its large, lobed fruit, seems to have been an American invention. There are tomatoes for cold and warm climates and for everywhere from hanging pots to thousand-acre farms whose soil is fumigated, mulched with plastic and irrigated with a virtually hydroponic solution of fertilizers and fungicides.

TOMATO BREEDERS

Traditionally, new tomato varieties came from selection: gardeners simply saved the seeds of the fruit they liked best. Over generations, an accumulation of small changes could add up to large differences. In the wild, too, tomatoes keep changing. It's a fact of evolution that not only do new strains arise slowly and inevitably but also new varieties or even species can appear quickly and dramatically when genes alter, resulting in what is known as a sport. Radiation can cause such a mutation—something now done in the laboratory. Yellow flesh, tangerine-colored flesh and pear-shaped fruits have arisen as sports in the wild. Determinate tomatoes, also called bush tomatoes—plants with a gene labeled "sp," for self-pruning—also began as sports. The sp gene appeared in Florida in 1914 and is now inherent in virtually all plants grown commercially in North America. Some additional sports have been induced in the laboratory by chemical mutagens.

Crossbreeding—controlling the romantic inclinations of tomato flowers—

has been the chief breeding technique for most of the 20th century. Choose a certain male flower to cross with a certain female on a different tomato plant, and you can produce a hybrid, a plant that may capitalize on the best of both parents to express vigor and size unseen in either. Hybrids can be advantageous for the short term but are unstable in the long run. Their seed will probably not produce a plant quite like either parent and may yield something very different, either better or worse. On the other hand, seeds saved from nonhybrids, also described as open-pollinated, will produce a new generation much like the previous one. It is this quality that ensures the continuing popularity of heirloom varieties, some of which, such as 'Mortgage Lifter' and 'Pineapple,' have been going strong for a century or more. Even heirloom tomatoes change gradually over generations, however, so the only way to grow an exact replica, a clone, of the parent is to reproduce it vegetatively, such as by taking a cutting.

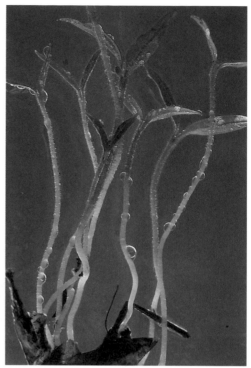

Heirloom tomato seedlings will produce fruit like that of their parents.

BRAVE NEW TOMATOES

Today, even the relatively new method of creating hybrids by crossing parent plants and checking out the offspring is too slow and imprecise for scientists pressured to increase harvests and profits at the same time as diseases become more prevalent and consumers more demanding. Certain goals in tomato breeding have remained constant over the centuries, whatever the breeding technique used. Healthy plants with lots of fruit have always been important. But the huge commercial industry that has arisen for both canning and the fresh market has a set of goals new to the 20th century, especially to the decades since machine harvesting began. More than 85 percent of the U.S. supply of processing tomatoes and more than 40 percent of the world supply is grown in California, which had completely converted to machine harvesting by the mid-1960s. The rest of the world has followed suit wherever human labor is more expensive than machines and fuel. Machines demand a very different tomato than what was sold in the Peruvian marketplace or even in Colonial America. Priorities today include uniform size for easy packing, resistance to bruising by machinery, simultaneous ripening for economical harvesting, a high content of solids for pastes and sauces and, for the fresh market types, slow ripening for long-distance shipping and tolerance to weeks of display in the supermarket.

The way to supply new tomatoes for these rapidly changing conditions is not just breeding; it is engineering. Genetic engineering, in which a donor gene is spliced into a recipient organism, is the latest way to create new cultivars—in fact, new mutagens, new sports. Any characteristic of a tomato plant can be altered by genetic engineering, and the genes can come from any living thing, not just another tomato. The multinational company Monsanto was the first to produce an economically successful genetically engineered tomato. Released in the late 1980s, it was resistant to tobacco mosaic virus. Varieties resistant to other diseases soon followed. In 1991, 20 percent of Monsanto's research and development budget was dedicated to biotechnology. It is technology that is both promising and frightening as humanity exchanges and rearranges the building blocks of life at competitive speed. One might wonder, How many genes can be borrowed from a petunia, a pepper, a pig, a fish before a tomato is no longer a tomato?

Robert Ambrose, publisher of *The Tomato Club* newsletter, a publication for home gardeners, is optimistic: "With genetic technology, it is only a matter of time before you are growing 3-pound, perfectly shaped, blemish-free, extremely flavorful tomatoes in your own backyard from plants which are resistant to disease, drought, heat and cold."

Whether or not he is right, it is certain that so far, no breeding technique has produced a delicious supermarket tomato. According to a survey reported in 1991, more than half of Americans buy no fresh tomatoes at all in winter. They fail to be enticed by the tough, almost tasteless fruits in the stores. That unconverted 50 percent of the population keeps the tomato-breeding industry frantic to discover a way to make a packable, shippable tomato that duplicates the taste and texture of summer

The End of the Line

Peter Henderson of Bergen, New Jersey, gives, in the *American Agriculturist*, a statement of his experiments with twenty-five of the varieties of tomato found in cultivation. He treated them all alike, transplanting three times as they advanced in growth. His observations brought him to the conclusion that the extreme point of earliness was reached some years ago; that the only improvement now to be made must be in size, smoothness or solidity; that the difference in time of maturity, of all the different kinds, does not exceed ten days at the farthest; that while the fruit may ripen in Georgia in May, in Virginia in June, in Delaware in July, and in New Jersey in August, a certain amount of heat is required to do the work.

—*The Illustrated Annual Register of Rural Affairs for 1871, Albany, New York*

fruit. One of the latest attempts, Calgene's genetically altered 'MacGregor's' tomato, supposedly able to deliver fresh flavor in winter, hit the market in the mid-1990s with much publicity but turned out to be mealy in texture and disappointing in flavor. Then, too, it cost two or three times the cost of other domestic tomatoes.

In the meantime, home gardeners continue to produce fruit fit for kings and queens, fresh off the vine in summer and frozen, dried or canned for winter. The supermarket does not tempt us. Our 'Early Girls' and 'Big Boys' are sultry and sun-kissed. They are as warm as a winter soup, as spicy as salsa, as child-friendly as ketchup, with just enough of a hint of a dangerous reputation to carry the love apple proudly into another millennium.

From Seed to Garden

What Do Tomatoes Want?

Where is Sigmund Freud the gardener when we need him? Or do we? There are plenty of home gardeners who grow perfectly good tomatoes without giving it much thought. Tomatoes are somewhat weedy plants with strong survival instincts. Given the right weather and soil conditions, they'll probably do fine. Just picture the slopes of the Andes mountains, where the ancestors of *Lycopersicon esculentum* survive with nary a human hand to help them. That environment, surely, represents what tomatoes want. Yet there's a big difference between leaving plants to their own devices and feeling pressured to grow a huge crop of perfect fruit. That's the situation for the commercial grower, who, to be as sure as possible of making a profit, wants the right cultivar, a soil analysis and a list of optimum temperatures and nutrients.

Fortunately, somewhere between wilderness and blind luck at one extreme and a costly analysis worthy of Freud the horticulturist at the other is the average home gardener. For us, seven points nicely sum up what tomatoes want. Here they are, though not necessarily in this order—tomatoes want all of these things, all at once:

1) WARMTH: Tomatoes do best at a consistent temperature range of about 50 to 85 degrees F, with days warmer than nights, though there are a few varieties known for their ability to put up with temperatures lower or higher. None can withstand prolonged cold or more than a brief exposure to frost.

2) FERTILITY: Tomatoes need enough nutrients in the right balance to sustain health and growth. Ordinary fertile

13

topsoil can supply these, but on the opposite end of the scale, tomatoes can be grown hydroponically with no soil at all, just a bath of nutrients in water. Commercial field growers opt for something between the two extremes.

3) WATER: Tomatoes must have enough fresh, warmish water to prevent wilting and to allow the fruit to fill out, but not so much that the plants drown.

4) BRIGHT LIGHT: For best fruit set, outdoor plants need a place exposed to the sun for at least half the day.

5) POLLINATION: For fruit, there must be something to pollinate the flowers. Outdoors, you needn't worry about this—a little wind will do it—but in the greenhouse, some attention has to be paid to pollination (page 71).

6) CALMNESS: Tomatoes need a location that is not constantly windy or frequently trampled.

7) FREEDOM FROM PESTS AND DISEASES: There should be as much protection as possible from all the things tomatoes *don't* want, which are described in Chapter 4.

There it is. Seven needs to keep in mind. Tomatoes are among the easiest vegetables you can grow.

TRANSPLANT OR SEED

The easiest way to start to grow them, the way most gardeners choose, is to buy young plants, called seedlings or transplants. In spring, garden stores and even supermarkets overflow with plastic packs of young tomatoes in the most popular varieties. Weather permitting, these may go straight into your garden.

If you choose to grow your tomatoes this way, skip over the next several paragraphs and pick up the directions again on page 18, under the heading "Hardening Off."

The alternative way to grow tomatoes is from seed. This is a little more complicated and means that the gardening season has to start some 6 to 8 weeks earlier than it would if you bought transplants. But growing from seed has a number of advantages that appeal to more experienced or adventurous gardeners. The chief one is cultivar selection. Racks of seed packets and mail-order catalogs offer scores of varieties. You can often find tomatoes especially bred to suit your climate and conditions, whether your season is short or long, cool or hot. Little-known or heirloom varieties have to be grown from seed. Want to try 'Yellow Pear'? 'Charlie's Red Staker'? 'Subarctic Maxi'? Want to enter a giant tomato contest? Order a few seed catalogs, and send in an order in winter or early spring.

Another advantage of seeds is that you can grow a large quantity of plants at little cost. An average packet contains 40 to 200 seeds for roughly the price you might pay for a six-pack of transplants. If you have a big garden, a big appetite for tomatoes or the urge to try something different, starting from seeds is probably the way to go.

There is a third way to grow tomatoes: from cuttings. To do this, you must have a large plant to start with, so for most gardeners, it is an option that arises only later in the season.

HYBRID VS. OPEN-POLLINATED

Whether you grow from seed or transplant, the varieties you choose may be hybrid or their opposite, called nonhybrid or open-pollinated. Older heirloom

Tomatoes can be grown from seed at home, like these 'Early Girls' in peat pots, or they can be bought as seedlings ready for outdoors.

types of tomatoes are all open-pollinated. Hybrids are more recent developments. Many have enhanced disease resistance, a feature that may make the difference between picking a good-size crop or a small one in your garden. Most gardeners don't mind whether the tomatoes they grow are hybrid or not. You are probably more concerned about flavor, fruit size and color and whether or not the tomato will ripen in your garden. But for some gardeners, this information is important, and while hybrid tomatoes are usually labeled as such, nonhybrid or open-pollinated tomatoes are not usually identified. It's a matter of omission: if a tomato is not called hybrid, chances are it's open-pollinated.

Gardeners who want to save their own seed prefer open-pollinated tomatoes, because their seeds should grow into plants much like the parents. You can also save the seeds of hybrids, but any tomatoes you grow from those seeds will probably not look just like the parents. In Chapter 3, tomatoes are classified as hybrid or open-pollinated.

BUSH VS. STAKING

There is another general classification for all tomatoes. They are recommended either for staking or for cages. These are actually two different types of plants. Scientists refer to staking tomatoes as indeterminate, because their eventual size and yield are not determined. Suckers that develop in all branch crotches will, length of season permitting, form blossoms and fruit. From indeterminates, you'll be picking fruit, a few at a time, till frost, but the first ripe fruit probably will not be ready till fairly late in the season. Many of the

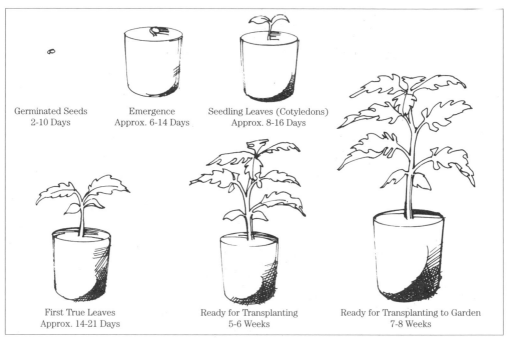

Germinated Seeds
2-10 Days

Emergence
Approx. 6-14 Days

Seedling Leaves (Cotyledons)
Approx. 8-16 Days

First True Leaves
Approx. 14-21 Days

Ready for Transplanting
5-6 Weeks

Ready for Transplanting to Garden
7-8 Weeks

All you need to see a tomato through its spring journey from seed to garden is a few pots, some sterilized soil and a warm, bright place indoors.

best-tasting varieties are indeterminates that require a long season. Indeterminates are also favored for greenhouses, because they make the best use of vertical space.

The second type, sometimes called bush or cage tomatoes, are determinate, because their ultimate size is determined. The vine terminates in a flower cluster, and plant growth slows after the fruits form. Determinates that have no more than one leaf between flower clusters are sometimes described as compact. Those with two leaves between flower clusters may be called semi-determinates, or vigorous determinates. Determinates should not be pruned, because they need all their leaves. This group includes most of the early varieties and virtually all paste tomatoes. It is the type preferred by commercial growers, because it produces one large crop of fruit, which makes harvesting economical and efficient. Determinates

need not be supported at all but can be allowed to sprawl on the ground.

LIGHT REQUIREMENTS

If you have chosen to grow your tomatoes from seed, you will be encouraged to know that tomatoes are among the easiest of garden candidates for indoor sowing. Given warmth and reasonable care, they should reward even the novice with success. They seldom suffer in transplanting, will grow new roots from their stems and, given the conditions they need, can often be revived even when they look nearly spent.

All you need is a warm, bright place, preferably in a greenhouse or under a light fixture that accommodates fluorescents alone or fluorescents in combination with incandescents. You don't need expensive lights, the types sold for flowering orchids or displaying houseplants. Ordinary cool white or warm

16

white fluorescents will do the job of raising healthy transplants, but the lights need to be close to the plant tops, just a couple of inches above, at all times. A facility that allows you to raise the lights or lower the plants will help keep the growing plants from being too far from the lights or touching them and burning. If you use lights, you must give the plants a rest of a few hours of darkness every night. Tomato plants suffer in continuous light. If you have neither greenhouse nor lights, a sunny windowsill can be used—that's all I use—but you must make sure seedlings do not become too leggy. Replanted more deeply in their pots, tomato seedlings that have become a bit leggy can be revived, but if they are really weak and pale, all is lost. Spindly, leaning plants arise from a combination of too much warmth with too little light. If the place is cool, then lower light can be tolerated. If the light is bright, more warmth is all right. On a window ledge, you can't adjust the light levels, so too much warmth is the usual culprit, especially when the thermostat is kept high even at night. A nighttime temperature of only about 60 degrees F makes for healthy seedlings. You can reduce legginess somewhat by shaking or rubbing the seedlings gently and giving them a quarter turn every day.

SOWING SEEDS

Seed pregermination helps get the crop off to a good start and avoids a glut of seedlings. This process should begin about 2 months before the last estimated spring frost date in your area. For most gardeners in the northern United States and Canada, that means pregerminating seeds around the end of March. On the Pacific Coast or farther south, you may be starting them in late January. To pregerminate, place a piece of paper toweling in the bottom of a flat-bottomed container, write the name of the tomato cultivar on the paper in ballpoint and dampen the towel with warm water. Pour off excess water. If you are growing several cultivars, you can divide the toweling into sections with your pen and write one of the cultivar names in each section. Spread your seeds sparsely in a single layer on the appropriate section—as many seeds as you want plants, plus another 10 to 20 percent to allow for germination failure and later losses. Leave the seeds uncovered, but close or cover the container and place it in a warm spot, preferably about 75 to 85 degrees F. Darkness is all right. Check every day to see whether any seeds have sprouted. If the paper towel dries, dampen it again. In a few days, the seeds will begin to germinate one at a time; you will see a small white rootlet emerging from the side. The seed is now ready to plant.

SEEDLING CONTAINERS

You can use any type of container at this point, provided it has a hole in the bottom to allow water to drain out. Plastic pots, polystyrene coffee cups and plastic dairy containers are all good. Brightly lit space is likely to be at a premium, so keep the containers fairly small, allowing each seed ½ to 1 inch of space all around. The cells of egg cartons can be used, but they hold so little soil, you will soon be transplanting again.

Seedlings are generally not grown in garden soil, which is too heavy for young roots to penetrate easily and comes complete with fungal diseases. Instead, most growers use a purchased mixture meant for seedlings. This sterile substance, free of disease organisms, is made up of peat moss, vermiculite

17

Planting tomatoes as deeply as the lowest leaves allows new roots to grow from the buried stem.

and other lightweight ingredients. You can make your own from a half-and-half mixture of potting soil and perlite or vermiculite. If you want to substitute your own compost for the potting soil in the mix, first sterilize it under boiling water to kill disease organisms.

Moisten the growing mix thoroughly with warm water, then fill the containers firmly. On the soil surface, press your finger about ¼ inch deep. Pick up a single germinated seed on your fingertip, and drop it into the depression. Cover the seed so that the soil surface is level, then water. Always use room-temperature water on tomato seedlings, never cold or hot. For now, the planted pots can stay in a dark place, provided it is warm.

Keep the soil damp until the little loops of emerging stems appear, then immediately place the containers in a well-lit spot, as described previously in this chapter. Once a week, give them a drink of liquid houseplant fertilizer at the dose recommended on the label. About 3 weeks before the last predicted spring frost, transplant the tomatoes into larger containers—milk cartons, juice cans or plant pots with drainage holes—one plant to a container. At this point, any good garden soil or compost

will do; it need not be sterilized. To transplant, tap the plant carefully from its first pot, complete with its entire root ball. If you have grown several seedlings in the same pot, you will have to separate them carefully, keeping as much soil as possible around each. Set each plant in its new pot more deeply than it grew before. Ideally, soil should now come up to the first true leaves, the lowest leaves that look serrated, like those of a mature tomato. The first leaves, or cotyledons, which are long and slender with smooth edges, will be underground, and new roots will emerge from the buried stem. Water well and set the containers back into their bright location. Now they can tolerate cooler days of 60 to 65 degrees F.

HARDENING OFF

From this point on, the growing procedure is the same whether you have purchased transplants or grown your own from seed. The only exception is if you have bought transplants that were displayed outdoors in full sun. These do not need hardening off and can be planted outdoors right away, but if the weather is not yet settled, they should be kept outdoors by day and brought indoors on cold nights.

With all other transplants, begin hardening them off about a week before your outdoor planting date by taking them outdoors on warm days, leaving them for an hour or so in a calm, shaded place, then bringing them in again. Every day, extend the outdoor stay and gradually introduce the plants to sun. After a few days, they can stay outdoors in their pots day and night. Of course, you will have to shelter them or bring them indoors if frost threatens or the weather is cold and windy, and once they are exposed to the sun and the open air, you must pay special attention to keeping them watered.

The timing of hardening off and planting depends on the weather. It is a shame to spend a lot of time growing seedlings only to have them die from a spell of cold weather or frost. When the soil feels warm and the temperature has become dependably pleasant, the plants can go into the ground, even if the average last spring frost date has not arrived, but you must be prepared to cover the plants if a frost warning does occur. You can plant earlier if you are using row covers or individual plant covers, described below.

AND SO TO BED

The soil for tomatoes should be at least a foot deep, rich in organic matter, such as compost, and about neutral or slightly acidic in pH. Soil-test kits that provide this information are available at garden stores in spring. As a general guideline, if you garden in a very dry area or where the bedrock is limestone, your soil is probably alkaline, and if you garden in a rainy area and the bedrock is not limestone, your soil is probably acidic.

Tomatoes should be planted in an area of the garden that is sunny, free of weeds and relatively calm. If you don't have a sunny place, you may still harvest fruit, just not as much of it. Opt for a cherry type rather than a large-fruited variety. Tomatoes can go into rows, into containers (see Chapter 5) or into beds. Raising the beds helps warm the soil and also makes the plants easier to reach. The easiest way to raise the beds is to rake the soil from the paths into mounds. For more permanent raised beds, the mounds can be bordered with boards, railway ties, concrete blocks or stones. If you have permanent raised beds, you will not be able to till the gar-

den as easily and your paths will need to be mowed grass or a hard material that can be kept free of weeds.

Planting into the garden is best done late in the day or when the weather is cool and calm, even a little rainy. Rake the bed fairly level. If you are planning to apply a plastic mulch—clear plastic dramatically warms the soil but allows weeds to grow underneath, while black plastic has less warming effect but keeps weeds in check—it should be in place before you plant and secured all around the edges. Cut an X in each spot where a tomato plant will go, allowing about 2 feet all around each plant.

Dig a hole big enough to accommodate the entire root ball as well as part of the stem. Tip the root ball out of the pot, and plant the tomato a little deeper than before, filling the hole around it with removed topsoil or with compost fortified with a handful of bonemeal. Give each plant a bucketful of tepid water, and press the soil firmly around the stem. Then nestle a cardboard circle or a tin can, both ends removed, about an inch into the ground around each stem to fend off cutworms.

PLANT COVERS

Tomatoes can be planted outdoors from 3 to 6 weeks earlier than normal if they can be kept warm in the garden. Warm soil is the most important necessity. A clear plastic mulch placed on the soil at least a week before planting time will raise the soil temperature by about 10 degrees F. In trials in Ontario, plastic mulch alone has advanced ripening by almost 3 weeks. It helps, too, to cover the plants whenever the weather is cooler than about 50 degrees. Entire rows or groups of plants can be covered with clear plastic or glass, or plants can be covered individually. Row covers are

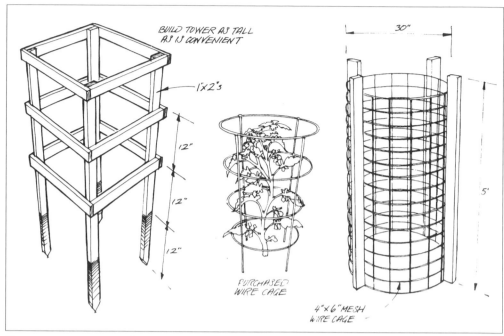

BUILD TOWER AS TALL AS IS CONVENIENT

1"x 2's

12"

12"

12"

PURCHASED WIRE CAGE

4"x 6" MESH WIRE CAGE

30"

5'

Tomato cages must be sturdy, with spaces for the branches to grow through.

most easily made by covering a series of #8- or #9-gauge wire hoops with sheets of transparent polyethylene. If you use row covers, you must mulch the ground with dark plastic or black paper to suppress weeds. The cover must be secured or buried all around the edges to hold it in place, and it must be slitted along the top to vent heat on sunny days. Too much heat is as damaging as too little—which is why the covers must be removed as soon as the outdoor weather is suitable for tomato growing, 1 or 2 weeks after your usual planting-out date for tomatoes. On a clear, sunny day, the temperature inside a slitted row cover can rise 20 to 30 degrees above the temperature outside.

Individual covers can vary from clear plastic bottles, their lids and bottoms removed, to purchased covers such as wax-paper or plastic hotcaps or Wall-O-Water, a double-sided, tubed plastic ring that holds water, retaining daytime heat around the plant at night. Researchers in Virginia who studied several different types of plant covers found the highest day temperatures and greatest frost protection with Wall-O-Water. The time to the first ripe fruit was reduced 11 days by Wall-O-Water, 7 days by a hot-cap and 5 days by a milk jug, as compared with unprotected plants.

A lightweight fabric cover such as Reemay also provides some extra warmth, though compared with clear polyethylene, this type of cover is less effective for heat retention and much more expensive. Reemay and other floating row covers are thus used to greater advantage as protection not from frost but from insects.

CAGES AND STAKES

If you intend to support the plants on stakes, insert them now, while you can still avoid the roots. Stakes should be at least 5 feet long, pounded 1 foot into the earth (2-by-2-inch lumber works well).

As the plants grow, twine the stems around the stakes or tie them loosely to their stakes with figure-eights of soft fabric or twine. There are other methods of holding plants upright:

SPIRAL STAKES: A galvanized-steel rod is fashioned into a 5-, 6- or 6½-foot-long spiral with a bottom spike that holds it upright. This unusual cage is available from The Natural Gardening Company. (See Sources, page 87.)

WATER STAKES: Dr. Stephen Reiners, technical editor of *The Tomato Club* newsletter, reported success with a piece of PVC pipe 6 feet long and 2 inches in diameter, buried 1 or 2 feet deep in the ground. It was important not to hammer the bottom end in but to bury it. Reiners suggests first hammering the pipe in, then removing it and shaking out the soil and, finally, placing it back in the same hole. Watering can then be done into the top of the stake, which holds 1 gallon of water and carries it down to the tomato roots. Fertilizers, too, can be poured into the water in the stake. Research has shown that tomato yields are highest when fertilizers go deep into the soil.

VERTICAL STRINGS: Lengths of strong twine that hang down from a crossbeam held on stout stakes can be twined around a tomato stem as it grows.

Tomatoes grown on stakes must have at least some of the suckers removed. These are shoots that grow in the crotches of branches of indeterminate tomatoes. Left to grow, each sucker is potentially a new fruit-bearing shoot that requires its own stake. Removing suckers will definitely lower the ultimate yield, but that won't matter if you've grown enough plants to com-

Stakes for indeterminate tomato plants should be at least 5 feet high.

pensate for the pruning. The general rule is that pruned plants produce larger fruits but fewer of them than plants left unpruned. Suckers pushed into the ground or into pots and kept watered will grow into new plants.

Some gardeners prune off foliage to hasten ripening, but ripening is a process that proceeds even in darkness. Pruning the foliage away is an invitation to sunscald and other fruit disorders.

Cages can be situated now too. Surrounding a cage with clear polyethylene will create a greenhouse environment that encourages growth in cool weather. The tall wire cages available commercially are sturdy enough only for medium- or small-size fruits. For plants with large, heavy fruit, consider making your own cages, round or square, from wood or wire. As plants grow, train them through the holes of their cages.

Another quite different sort of support has been described as resembling an old army cot. Upright stakes about 2 feet long are attached to a horizontal, rectangular frame of 2-by-2 wood the length and width of the tomato bed (or whatever size is convenient). Chicken wire is stretched tightly across the horizontal frame and stapled or nailed in place. Then the uprights are set a foot deep into the perimeter of the tomato bed. The plants grow through the chicken wire and then spread out over it, so the fruit is kept off the ground and plants need not be pruned.

MULCHING

All tomatoes should be mulched. One of the most important benefits of any mulch is that it keeps pathogens in the soil from splashing onto lower leaves. Second, all mulches help retain soil moisture while limiting weed growth. But there are other benefits. Determinate, or bush, tomatoes allowed to sprawl on the ground will stay clean on a mulch of either plastic or an organic substance such as grass clippings, seaweed or hay. Plastic mulches should be in place before the plants go into the garden, as described above. Organic mulches are quite different. They should not be applied for about 2 weeks after spring planting, because they slow the warming of the soil, which is important for quick growth. Wait till after a rain or a thorough watering when the plants are about a foot or more tall, then apply 3 or 4 inches of organic mulch or whatever you can manage.

FERTILIZING

Tomatoes growing on ordinary soil should require no extra fertilizing at all, though you may want the insurance of one of the fertilizers specially blended for tomatoes. Do not apply too much nitrogen (in a form such as manure, blood meal, cottonseed meal or any fertilizer with a high first number in its analysis), or you will encourage the growth of leaves at the expense of fruit and might promote diseases.

WATERING

Tomatoes should not be allowed to wilt, yet they do not like constantly wet ground. They grow best in well-drained soil given 1 to 1½ inches of water a week. If possible, don't water the leaves, an invitation to fungal diseases, but apply the water directly on or under the ground. If you have just a few plants, the best plan is to use a watering can and water thoroughly by hand whenever the top inch or so of the soil feels dry. Inserting a large can, both ends removed, next to each plant will allow you to fill the can, whose contents will then slowly percolate to plant roots. Water stakes, described on page 21, have the same effect. The advantage of any of these hands-on watering methods is that you

Giant Tomatoes

The following list is condensed from Miracle-Gro's suggestions for winning its annual Giant Tomato Challenge, which carries a grand prize of $100,000.

1. Choose a variety of seed that produces big tomatoes, such as 'Big Boy,' 'Big Girl,' 'Beefmaster,' 'Supersteak,' 'Giant Belgium,' 'German Johnson' or 'Whopper.'

2. Wait till frost has passed and the soil temperature is about 65 degrees F before planting your tomatoes outdoors.

3. Give your plants a place where they will receive a minimum of 8 hours a day of sun; full sun all day is better. The soil should be well-drained loam or sandy loam, preferably rich in organic matter. The pH should be 6 to 6.5.

4. Plant your seedlings at least 3 feet apart in all directions—4 feet is better. Mulch with peat, compost, grass clippings, newspapers or plastic sheeting.

5. Give the plants an inch of water a week. Feel the soil 1 or 2 inches below the surface; if it's dry, give the plants a moderate soaking.

6. Fertilize plants once or twice a week. If you intend to enter the contest, you must use Miracle-Gro on your tomatoes.

7. Use sturdy stakes or wire cages, and support plants with soft material such as cotton rags or panty hose. Don't use wire or common cord.

8. Prune the plant, allowing only one stem to develop. Prune off the lower branches to at least 18 inches above the ground. Remove all suckers, but don't remove leaves except where necessary. After a few fruits have formed, choose three of the largest, particularly those on the lower branches, and pinch off all remaining fruit and all the blossoms. After about 2 weeks, select the best and biggest of the three, and remove the other two fruits. Meanwhile, don't let any new tomatoes form—just keep pinching off the blossoms.

To win the Giant Tomato Challenge, the tomato must weigh more than the current record holder, 7 pounds 12 ounces, grown by Gordon Graham of Oklahoma in 1987. He grew a variety named 'Delicious.' For a list of the rules, write Miracle-Gro Tomato Challenge, c/o Nationwide Consumer Testing Institute, 1415 Park Avenue, Hoboken, NJ 07030.

can use ambient-temperature water collected in a rain barrel or allowed to sit till it reaches air temperature. Tap water is usually cold, and cold water slows down tomato root growth.

For a large area of tomatoes, you may want to invest in trickle or drip irrigation. In these systems, water trickles or seeps out of a hose placed on or under the soil surface near the plants. Only the ground is watered, and water use is more efficient because less water is lost to evaporation. A soaker hose utilizes tiny pores, whereas trickle tape, the type used by commercial growers, has emitters or holes spaced as far as every 2 feet. Trickle tape is less likely to clog if your water is hard or muddy. There are various suppliers for these watering systems. (See Sources, page 87.)

For the next few weeks, the principal jobs include weeding, protecting the plants from frost, watering regularly during drought and watching for pests and signs of disease. If the plants become yellowish, cool weather may be to blame. Continue weeding, watering and fertilizing as needed, and begin to harvest the fruit as soon as it is slightly soft and fully colored.

Kinds and Considerations

The Favorite Tomatoes for Home Gardens

The following is a list of the best-selling tomatoes offered by North American seed catalogs. They are divided into the categories of cherry, medium-size, large, paste and unusual. Within those categories, there are varieties for cold places and hot, for small gardens and large. The following terminology is included in the descriptions:

HYBRID OR OPEN-POLLINATED: Listed as H or OP after each description. These terms are defined in Chapter 2.

DETERMINATE OR INDETERMINATE: These two groups of tomatoes are defined in Chapter 2.

DISEASE RESISTANCE: Tomatoes with inbred disease or pest resistance (when known) are given the following initials after the variety name: A, Alternaria (early blight); C, Clodisporium (leaf mold); F, Fusarium wilt, race 1; FF, Fusarium wilt, races 1 and 2; N, Nematodes; S, Stemphylium (gray leaf spot); T, Tobacco Mosaic Virus; V, Verticillium wilt.

DAYS TO MATURITY: The number of days listed at the end of each variety description refers to the length of time from outdoor transplanting to first harvest. This duration is dependent upon weather and the size and health of the transplant, so it is best considered as a means of comparing one variety with another. These dates are taken from seed catalogs. Where the catalogs disagree, the earliest and latest suggested dates are listed.

ALL-AMERICA SELECTIONS (AAS): Tomatoes that have won this award have excelled in trials across the United States

25

and Canada. The trials are aimed at determining the best varieties for home gardens in all climatic areas.

HEIRLOOM: An open-pollinated tomato of some vintage. Many date back to the 1800s or earlier.

CHERRY TOMATOES

(Average fruit weighs less than 2 ounces)

Chello

"Most yellow cherry tomatoes are grown more for color than for good taste, but 'Chello' has both: excellent sweet tomato flavor and jewel-like, golden yellow fruits," says Shepherd's. 'Chello's' bright yellow, inch-wide fruits are borne on a small, bushy determinate plant well suited to a sunny container or window box. OP. 60 to 63 days.

Cherry Gold

Compact determinate plants only 6 inches high and wide are recommended for small pots and indoor windowsills. The fruit is extremely early. "A golden version of 'Tiny Tim,' better flavored," says Stokes. OP. 45 days.

Gardener's Delight (Sugar Lump)

This heirloom cherry produces clusters of golf-ball-sized, crack-resistant fruits on indeterminate vines. One of the parents of 'Sweet 100,' this old-timer bears fruit less sweet, but some people prefer the more characteristic tomato flavor. OP. 60 to 65 days.

Gold Nugget (Golden Nugget)

A variety developed at Oregon State University, this determinate cherry sets fruit well even in cool weather. "Rich, sweet flavor," reports the Tomato Growers Supply Company. The deep golden fruit is approximately an inch wide and

Possibly the sweetest cherry of all, 'Sweet Million' is also disease-resistant.

almost seedless early in the season. OP. 56 to 60 days.

Large Red Cherry (Red Cherry)

A favorite of southern growers who want to save their own seed, this indeterminate bears clusters of large, 1½-inch cherry fruits with a sweet, mild flavor. In experiments in Alabama in 1989, 'Red Cherry' had the highest yields despite maximum summer temperatures that are much too hot for most varieties, between 88 and 102 degrees F. OP. 70 to 75 days.

Red Robin

Tiny 8-to-12-inch-tall determinate plants bearing masses of red fruit a little wider than an inch are recommended for containers indoors and out. "Outstanding flavor plus attractive display in hanging baskets, windowsills and

Vigorous indeterminate vines produce grapelike clusters of 'Sweet 100.'

patio planters make this a winner!" says Park Seeds. OP. 63 days.

Santa
Similar to 'Teardrop,' with unusually shaped oval fruit in clusters on indeterminate vines. A Thompson & Morgan 1997 news release says, "Firm and well textured with exceptional flavor—juicy and supremely sweet, but with a hint of that famous tomato tang." H. 75 days.

Small Fry VFN
An AAS winner in 1970, this 40-inch-tall determinate bears clusters of bright red 1-inch fruit. It can be grown in cages but is recommended by Stokes for hanging baskets. H. 60 to 72 days.

Sugar Snack NT
Similar to 'Sweet 100,' this 1997 release from Ball Seed Company bears long clusters of sweet 1-ounce fruits on indeterminate vines. Yields are higher than with similar varieties, and the tomatoes retain their high quality longer in the garden. Heavy foliage protects the fruit from sunscald. H. 65 days.

Sun Gold FT (Sungold)
This Japanese variety bears large clusters of crack-resistant, rich orange-colored cherries with what Johnny's calls "a yummy 'tropical' or 'winey' taste" on strong, indeterminate vines. "One of the first tomatoes to bear in our gardens," writes The Cook's Garden, "but still a favorite even after the main crops come in." H. 57 to 65 days.

Supersweet 100 VF (Super Sweet 100 VF)
"Sweeter and more disease-resistant than 'Sweet 100,' " says Park's 1996 catalog, "but with the same great flavor and amazingly high yields of 1-inch fruits." The fruits on this indeterminate have a very high vitamin C content. H. 60 to 65 days.

Sweet Chelsea VFNT
An indeterminate with larger—almost 2-inch—more crack-resistant fruit than 'Sweet 100' has, but similarly sweet. Again, the fruit is borne in huge clusters. Plants grow about 3 feet tall. H. 67 days.

Sweet Million FNTS
More disease-resistant than 'Sweet 100' is, with larger, darker red fruit more resistant to cracking but otherwise similar, with fruit produced in clusters on indeterminate vines. "The sweetest tomato in our trials," says Jung. "We guarantee you will find yourself eating these little treats like candy." H. 60 to 65 days.

Sweet 100
Named for its enormous yield of sugary cherry fruits, 'Sweet 100' is still the first

Grown in a small pot, 'Tiny Tim' will ripen its inch-wide cherry fruit even on a sunny windowsill.

choice of many gardeners, although it has been surpassed in disease and crack resistance. Fruit grows in grapelike clusters on a vigorous indeterminate vine. If not staked, it will ramble a long distance. The fruits are high in vitamin C. H. 60 to 65 days.

Sweet Orange FT
An indeterminate with brick-red, firm, round, inch-wide fruit, crack- and disease-resistant. H. 60 days.

Sweetie
A sprawling indeterminate that produces clusters of sweet, cherry-sized, red fruit about 70 days from transplanting, much like 'Sweet 100' but not hybrid, so seeds can be saved. "An open-pollinated alternative to the many hybrids available," says William Dam.

"Recommended unless you have problems with diseases." OP. 65 to 75 days.

Teardrop
Unusual oval-shaped fruit, dark red, almost seedless and just over an inch long, "with unique flavor, rich fragrance and nonsplitting skin," says Park Seeds. Indeterminate vines produce fruit in huge clusters. H. 60 days.

Tiny Tim
A determinate released by the University of New Hampshire in 1945 is still favored for small pots, hanging baskets and indoor windowsills because of its short stem, about 15 inches long, and fruit less than an inch wide. On the negative side, 'Tiny Tim' is tough-skinned and not the best for flavor. OP. 45 to 55 days.

Toy Boy VF
A determinate excellent for small gardens, pots or hanging baskets. The plants grow only 12 to 14 inches tall, with plenty of 1½-inch red fruit. The Tomato Growers Supply Company advises, "Grow 3 or 4 plants in one 10-inch container." H. 68 days.

MEDIUM-SIZE TOMATOES
(Average fruit weighs 2 to 10 ounces)

Arkansas Traveler
This southern indeterminate heirloom, developed before 1900, has "traveled" all over the south from its origins in Arkansas. Everywhere it goes, it is appreciated for good crops of 6-to-8-ounce pink fruit despite drought and hot weather. OP. 85 days.

Bonny Best
It won't win any trials for productivity or flavor, but this old-fashioned variety still commands a following. Indeterminate

Many of the favorite North American garden tomatoes are beefsteaks, whose name comes from their irregular, flattened shape and solid, meaty texture.

vines bear fruit as large as 8 ounces. 76 days. William Dam sells 'Bonny Best Improved,' "one of the best medium early varieties." OP. 70 days.

Bush Beefsteak
A favorite where summers are short, this open-pollinated, compact, bushy determinate yields ½-pound, rich red, solid beefsteak fruit. OP. 62 to 65 days.

Bush Early Girl VFNT
New in 1997, this determinate is similar to 'Early Girl' in fruit size, color and flavor but has better disease resistance. Red fruits average 6½ to 7½ ounces. H. 54 days.

Cabot
Popular in New England and the Maritime Provinces, this determinate is a dwarf open plant that produces medium-size fruit which ripens to brilliant red in about 68 days. OP.

California Sun VFN
Indeterminate but dwarf, just 3 or 4 feet tall, and thus ideal for containers or

29

'Celebrity' combines high yields and good size with disease resistance.

A French beauty noted for good flavor is the indeterminate 'Dona.'

small gardens. Tasty 7- or 8-ounce fruit ripens till season's end. H. 70 days.

Campbell 1327 VF
This determinate, especially recommended for the northeastern states, is popular for canning because its large, 7-ounce flattened fruit is firm and rich red. It is crack-resistant and sets heavy crops even when the weather is unfavorable. There is good foliage cover. OP. 70 to 75 days.

Carnival VFFNTA
"A most impressive early-ripening hybrid beefsteak-type tomato," says Vesey's. "Outstanding flavor, yield and disease resistance." A companion to 'Celebrity,' 'Carnival' has similar fruit, but the determinate vines are shorter and bushier. H. 70 to 72 days.

Caro Rich
This and its companion 'Caro Red' were produced at Purdue University for a high vitamin A content. Seeds of Change says, "A low-acid variety with delicious, sweet flavor. Good production in cooler climates." Although the vines

are indeterminate, they grow only about 2 feet tall. The orange tomatoes are 3 or 4 inches wide. OP. 80 days.

Celebrity VFFNTA
This 1984 AAS winner has remained popular from coast to coast because of superior disease resistance and a high production of good-size, tasty, 6-to-10-ounce, deep red fruits despite the weather. The determinate plants are strong and need cages or poles for support. H. 70 to 76 days.

Champion VFNT
An indeterminate "especially bred as a luscious sandwich tomato," says the Tomato Growers Supply Company. 'Champion' offers "solid, meaty slices with just the right sweetness. High yields of large fruit, bigger than 'Early Girl' and earlier than 'Better Boy.' Outstanding performer." H. 70 days.

Creole
This indeterminate was developed in Louisiana for tolerance to hot, humid weather. The fruit is red, smooth and firm, with strong flavor and plenty of

juice. Resistant to fusarium wilt and blossom-end rot. Grow it in a cage or tied to a stake. OP. 78 days.

Dona VFFNT
Appreciated for its good flavor in France, where it originated, this indeterminate bears large, early crops of red, 4-to-6-ounce, slightly flattened fruit. "A choice tomato for beauty, quality and, above all, rich, mouth-filling flavor," says Shepherd's. H. 65 to 75 days.

Doublerich (Double Rich)
Bred by North Dakota State University to have twice the usual amount of vitamin C—"as much as oranges," according to Seeds of Change—this 2-to-4-foot indeterminate bears 7-ounce red tomatoes that are resistant to cracking. "The meat is bright red, solid and meaty (but juicy). Not that many seeds. Good for canning and juices," says Bountiful Gardens. OP. 60 to 80 days.

Early fruit of high quality comes in abundance from 'Early Cascade.'

Early Cascade VF
Named for its early production of bright red fruit in cascades or trusses, like grapes, this Petoseed Company indeterminate is best for gardens where the season is short. "An outstanding hybrid for home or commercial growers, as it sets and produces numerous firm, rich red, medium-size tomatoes," says Vesey's. "Strong support is necessary. Prune side shoots to leave only one or two main stalks per plant." H. 55 to 65 days.

Early Girl VFF
Enduringly popular and available from almost every catalog, this Ball Seed Company release produces red, 4-to-6-ounce, globe-shaped fruit. Relatively early production and continuous bearing make it especially favored where the season is short. "Our earliest slicing tomato," says Park Seeds. Indeterminate plants grow tall, so they should be staked or caged. H. 52 to 64 days.

Enchantment VFFN
Three-inch oval fruits, the type called "saladette," grow in clusters on vigorous indeterminate vines. "Their unique shape and firm but juicy texture makes them perfect tomatoes to eat out of hand, cut into perfect oval slices or cook into the thick sauce consistency every cook appreciates," writes Shepherd's. "They have a well-balanced sugar-to-acid ratio that translates into full-bodied tomato flavor." The Tomato Growers Supply Company says this is one of the first tomatoes to have resistance to bacterial speck. H. 68 to 70 days.

Fantastic
An indeterminate developed by the Petoseed Company, with smooth, 31

'Floramerica' offers dependability.

round, red fruit, 6 to 8 ounces. The immature fruits have prominent green shoulders. Texture is fine and flavor is good. It is fairly early and bears heavily throughout the season. H. 70 to 72 days.

First Lady VFFNT
An early indeterminate with 4-to-6-ounce, smooth, crack-resistant fruit, deep red inside and out, on disease-resistant plants. "A breakthrough," writes Jung, "this extra-early hybrid puts the emphasis on flavor, and this is simply one of the most flavorful tomatoes we've ever tasted." William Dam says, "An improved 'Early Girl' type with crack-resistant, firm, bright red tomatoes." Johnny's also recommends this for greenhouses. H. 60 to 65 days.

Floramerica VFFA
A 1978 All-America winner developed by the University of Florida with toler-

ance or resistance to 15 diseases and disorders. "It will produce large crops where others fail," Jung says. Yields are high, and the large, scarlet fruit has excellent flavor for fresh use, canning or juicing. The strong determinate is adapted to a wide range of growing conditions. H. 70 to 75 days.

Gardener VF
Developed by Dr. Henry Munger at Cornell about 1972, this variety is early, with a tart, sweet flavor. The fruit is a little under 2 inches wide. "It may be picked in the pink stage for later ripening to red with minimal loss of quality," writes Southern Exposure Seed Exchange. "Recommended for northern gardeners as a main-crop tomato." OP. 63 days.

Glacier
This is valued for its ability to produce a crop of 3-ounce red fruit even in cool weather. Results of *HortIdeas* magazine's trial of open-pollinated varieties in Kentucky stated that 'Glacier' "outgrew early blight to continue producing late in the season. It was indeterminate and quite vigorous, with good-tasting medium-size fruit." OP. 62 days.

Glamour
One of the first crack-resistant varieties, this indeterminate came out of the Bird's-Eye Company in New York. It is also verticillium-tolerant and bears 6-to-8-ounce round, red, tasty fruit. OP. 75 days.

Hawaiian VFNT
A favorite of many Southerners, this indeterminate is heat-tolerant. The 10-ounce red fruit is smooth, firm and delicious. H. 70 days.

Heatwave VFFA
As its name suggests, this is one of the best choices for places where daytime

Gardeners who want 'Marglobe' should search for improved selections.

temperatures climb to 96 degrees F. The determinate bears abundant crops of 7-ounce red fruit. H. 68 days.

Husky series
'Husky Gold' VF was an All-America Selection. What distinguishes this plant and its 'Husky' cousins is that these are dwarf indeterminates. As the Liberty catalog notes, "Previous dwarf types were determinates that set fruit early, then quit. 'Husky Gold' sets fruit continuously right up to frost." The foliage is unusually heavy and wrinkled. There is a thick central stem about 4 feet tall. Plants are suited to containers but need a stake or cage to support the 5-to-7-ounce orange fruit of 'Husky Gold' VF, 70 days; red fruit of 'Husky Red' VF, 68 days; or pink fruit of 'Husky Pink' VF, 70 days. There are also two cherry tomatoes in the series.

Jet Star VF
An indeterminate developed by the Harris Seed Company and favored by many gardeners for its mild flavor, it is too low in acid to be recommended for safe canning. The 8-ounce red fruit is borne in large quantities and generally free of cracks. The vine is compact, and foliage cover is good. H. 72 days.

Johnny's 361 VFFNT
Judged one of the best-tasting tomatoes by *The Tomato Club* newsletter, this 1990 introduction from Johnny's Selected Seeds has another advantage: it does well where summers are cool. It is a determinate with 8-ounce, red, beefsteak-type fruit. H. 64 days.

Lemon Boy VFN
This was the first tomato colored not golden but lemon-yellow inside and out. The mild-flavored fruit, about 7 ounces, is produced on indeterminate plants that need support. H. 70 to 72 days.

Manalucie F
A southern favorite because it is disease-resistant and the upright, leafy indeterminate vines offer good protection from sunscald. Seven-ounce fruits are meaty and thick-walled. In *HortIdeas* magazine's 1985 trial of open-pollinated varieties in Kentucky, the judges rated its taste only "fair" and noted "moderate early-blight symptoms, nothing special." OP. 80 to 83 days.

Manitoba
Developed at the Agriculture Canada station in Morden, Manitoba, and described by Stokes as a "far north beefsteak," this determinate, a favorite of Canadian prairie gardeners, produces big crops of brick-red, slightly flattened 6-to-7-ounce fruit. OP. 60 days.

Marglobe VF (Marglobe Improved)
The original 'Marglobe,' a cross between 'Marvel' and 'Globe' released by the USDA in 1925, stayed popular for decades. Determinate plants bear 5-to-8-ounce firm red fruits with good flavor.

Hubbard Eclipsed

J. Peirson of Genesee County, New York, who raises annually many acres of tomatoes for canning, finds the two best to be 'Conqueror' and 'Hathaway,' the former proving as early or earlier than the 'Hubbard'—larger, smoother and a better grower. They were beginning to ripen in the open ground about the middle of July. The best crops of tomatoes yield 400 bushels per acre; none go below 200 bushels.

—*The Illustrated Annual Register of Rural Affairs for 1877, Albany, New York*

Unfortunately, in trials by *HortIdeas* magazine in Kentucky, the original was so prone to disease that production dropped to almost nothing late in the season, and the tomato was summed up as "nothing special." This newer disease-resistant selection is offered by Southern Exposure. OP. 67 days.

Marmande VF (Super Marmande)

A French semi-determinate heirloom known for good flavor and the ability to bear well in cool weather. It bears 5-to-8-ounce, beefsteak-shaped, scarlet fruit. "We think this is the best tomato of the beefsteak type," says Bountiful Gardens, who recommends it for outdoors or under glass. *HortIdeas* magazine came up with quite a different opinion from trials in Kentucky: "Good for gardens with early-blight problems—too bad the taste isn't better!" William Dam gives an alternative name, 'Vleestomaat,' and includes it among the paste types. OP. 62 to 67 days.

Miracle Sweet VFFNT

New in 1996, this indeterminate yields very large crops of 4-to-5-ounce tomatoes that are smooth and uniformly red on vigorous plants. "Outstanding flavor in an early, tremendously productive tomato," says the Tomato Growers Supply Company. H. 67 days.

Monte Carlo VFN

Large, beautiful fruits grow on strong indeterminate vines that are widely adaptable. "Excellent flavor and resistance to cracking, catfacing, sunscald and blossom-end rot," says the Tomato Growers Supply Company. In taste tests at the Alabama Agricultural Experiment Station, this one and 'Better Boy' ranked highest. 'Monte Carlo' also outyielded many others. H. 75 days.

Mountain series

These hybrid determinates were developed by Dr. Randy Gardner of the University of North Carolina. All can be grown on short stakes or in cages or allowed to sprawl. 'Mountain Delight' VFFA is the earliest, at about 69 to 73 days, and fruits average about half a pound. "Juicy, rich-flavored," says Park Seeds. 'Mountain Gold' VFF has been called a yellow-fruited sister to 'Mountain Delight.' The fruit is large and crack-resistant, with a mild flavor. 71 days. 'Mountain Pride' VFF has larger, firm fruit in 75 days. 'Mountain Fresh' VF has slightly larger, crack-resistant fruit but matures later, around 76 days. "Flavor has been rated superior to both 'Mountain Pride' and 'Mountain Delight,'" says the Tomato Growers Supply Company. 'Mountain Pride' VF is the latest, at 77 days, with smaller, 6-ounce fruit of top quality, though the plants are less disease-resistant than 'Mountain Delight.' 'Mountain Spring' VFF has the largest fruit, about 9 ounces in 72 days. The texture softens with ripening. 'Mountain Supreme' VF has comparable flavor to 'Mountain Pride' and 'Mountain Delight,' but the fruit is a little smaller. 'Mountain Gold' VFF bears 9-ounce orange fruit in about 72 days. All are hybrid.

New Yorker V
An old favorite among open-pollinated red tomatoes, 'New Yorker' produces good-size, 6-ounce red fruit on very small determinate plants. The largest fruit ripens within about 10 days, after which the fruit size decreases markedly. OP. 63 to 64 days.

Oregon Spring V
"The solution for all the frustrated coastal and short-season gardeners we've been hearing from," says Shepherd's, "'Oregon Spring's' heavy yields of rich-tasting ripe tomatoes will satisfy you at last!" Bred at Oregon State University, this compact, cold-tolerant determinate is popular with Westerners, because the fruit comes early and in good quantities. Johnny's also recommends it for planting early under row covers. OP. 58 days.

Patio F
A determinate that grows only about 2 feet tall, large enough to need a stake but small enough for a 12-inch pot or several to a half-barrel. The plant is treelike, similar to 'Husky,' but with smaller fruit, about 4 ounces, oval, red and flavorful. The foliage resembles that of potatoes. H. 50 to 65 days.

Peron
"Our pride and joy," says Gleckler's. Sometimes dubbed "the sprayless tomato," this indeterminate has a reputation for inbred pest resistance. The 8-ounce red fruit is high in vitamin C. "Very dependable, an excellent producer," writes Seeds Blüm. In its Kentucky trials, *HortIdeas* magazine rated 'Peron' as "very good flavor, a good

tomato," but listed its maturation date at 82 days, rather than the usual 68 days. OP.

Pik-Red VF
"The most popular variety in the Hume household," according to the Ed Hume catalog, this bushy determinate, 4 feet tall, produces medium-size beefsteak fruit despite cool weather. It is named for its almost solid-red fruit that is favored by small commercial growers because it can be picked ripe to ship to local markets without damage. The sturdy dwarf vines can be planted closer together than many others can. H. 71 days.

Pixie II
A more disease-resistant version of 'Pixie,' a small-fruited determinate meant for growing in pots. Plants grow no taller than 18 inches, with smooth, meaty fruit just under 2 inches wide. William Dam also recommends it for hydroponics and indoors. OP. 52 days.

Quick Pick VFFNTA
Heavy yields of round, red tomatoes on trouble free indeterminate vines. "An outstanding variety with medium-size, smooth fruit of excellent flavor and texture," says the Tomato Growers Supply Company. II. 60 days.

Ruby Cluster VFF
New from Johnny's in 1997, this indeterminate resembles 'Early Cascade,' with 2- or 3-ounce round, red fruit in clusters of 8 to 10. The flavor is improved. H. 60 days.

Rutgers (Rutgers Improved)
Developed by the Campbell Soup Company in 1928 and further refined by Rutgers University in 1943, this determinate is still popular because, as Bountiful Gardens says, "it has fantastic old-time

'Rutgers' offers old-fashioned flavor.

flavor." Wilt- and rust-resistant vigorous vines produce 6-to-8-ounce smooth fruit, free of cracks and especially valued for canning. The plant does well in high humidity. "Vigorous and prolific, meaty, bright red," writes Seeds Blüm. Liberty Seed Company offers 'Rutgers PS-R,' which is resistant to fusarium and verticillium wilt. H. 74 to 80 days.

Scotia
"Used to make Maritime green-tomato relish by customers in New Brunswick, Nova Scotia and Maine," Stokes says. This open-pollinated determinate, developed in Nova Scotia, has smooth, firm, green-shouldered, 4-ounce, tasty fruit that, despite cool coastal weather, ripens red in about 60 days. OP.

Siberia (Siberian)
The advantage here is earliness and tolerance to cool weather, as the name suggests. 'Siberia,' which originated in the former Soviet Union, can set fruit at lower temperatures than do most others, but the flavor is bland compared with that of later varieties. In *HortIdeas* magazine's Kentucky trials of open-pollinated tomatoes, the judges reported, "It might be good for the north but one of the poorest tomatoes we've tried here." Fruit is 3 to 4 ounces, red, on 2-to-3-foot wind-resistant determinate plants. OP. 55 to 69 days.

Solar Set VFF
A heat-tolerant determinate developed at the University of Florida, this plant sets fruit well even when humidity is high and nights are warm. Bright red, 8-to-9-ounce fruit has "a delicious, full tomato flavor," the Tomato Growers Supply Company says. "Great for a fall crop in areas where weather permits." H. 70 days.

Spitfire VFF
A growers' favorite because it ships well, 'Spitfire' also suits home gardeners where fall comes early, for the 8-ounce tomato resists cracking and ripens from the inside out. "Pick this tomato when it looks half ripe, cut it open, and you'll be delighted to find juicy, sweet red meat," Jung writes of this vigorous determinate. OP. 68 days.

Spring Giant VFN
The first tomato to become an All-America Selection (in 1967), this determinate produces a big crop of large, bright red, almost coreless fruits in a concentrated harvest season. Fruits may suffer from sunscald, so should be protected in cages. H. 65 days.

Starfire
A release from the Agriculture Canada station at Morden, Manitoba, this de-

'Siberia's' only advantages are earliness and cold tolerance; in warmer gardens, it is eclipsed in flavor, yield and quality by most other varieties.

terminate is a compact, bushy plant with good-size, 6-to-8-ounce red beefsteak fruit. It is especially recommended for sandy soils between the 40th and 50th parallels. OP. 56 days.

Stupice
"A garden mainstay," Southern Exposure writes. "Fruits have a depth of flavor, with a wonderful balance of sweetness and tartness." This cold-tolerant dwarf indeterminate from Czechoslovakia bears clusters of 2-ounce fruit that is red with an orange undertone, with some green shoulders late in the season. The Tomato Growers Supply Company reports, "In a 1988 variety test in the San Francisco Bay area, 'Stupice' rated first in flavor and production; an average 87 fruits were picked per plant." OP. 52 to 70 days.

Sub Arctic Maxi
"Earliest tomato for home gardens," William Dam says. This Canadian release has the largest fruit of the 'Sub Arctic' series of extremely early varieties meant for cold places. The red

fruits, about 2½ ounces, grow on small, open, determinate plants. OP. 48 days.

Sunbeam VFFA

New in 1996, this determinate produces 10-ounce, bright red, attractive fruit favored for roadside sales. The vigorous, high-quality plants have done especially well in the eastern United States. H. 70 to 74 days.

Super Chief VF

This determinate from South Dakota State University has bright red 8-ounce fruits, larger than most tomatoes this early. The Tomato Growers Supply Company writes, "In a 5-year comparison trial, yields of 'Super Chief' surpassed both 'Celebrity' and 'Better Boy.'" H. 65 days.

Supersonic VF

An indeterminate developed by the Harris Seed Company, which produces large harvests of meaty, 9-ounce red tomatoes with a solid structure tolerant to cracking. Especially popular in the northeastern states. The Tomato Growers Supply Company recommends that its vigorous, leafy vines be confined in a cage. H. 79 days.

Trip-L-Crop (Climbing; Italian Tree)

Not really a climber, though sometimes advertised as such, this indeterminate variety can reach 10 feet in a season, bearing potatolike foliage and large yields of 3-by-5-inch, oval red fruit. It must be staked or grown on a tall trellis or fence. OP. 85 days.

Tropic VFN

Often grown in greenhouses, this indeterminate variety has such dependable disease resistance that it is also a favorite in hot, humid, disease-prone places, especially in the mid-Atlantic states. The 8- or 9-ounce fruit is thick-walled and red with slightly green shoulders. Good foliage cover helps protect it from sunscald. "A number of our customers have been very pleased with the resistance of this variety to blight," Southern Exposure notes. OP. 81 days.

Wonder Boy VFN

This nematode-resistant improvement replaced the original 'Wonder Boy' years ago. It bears 8-ounce, meaty tomatoes with delicious flavor. The strong-growing indeterminate vines offer good foliage cover for protection against sunscald. H. 80 days.

LARGE TOMATOES

(Average fruit weighs 12 ounces or more)

Abraham Lincoln (Early Abraham Lincoln)

The name Abraham Lincoln has been used for tomatoes more than once. The original was a late indeterminate released in 1923 from Buckbee's seed farm in Illinois. It had bronze-tinted foliage. The variety mostly available now, developed around 1975, is earlier than the original, with clusters of 1- or 2-pound, bright red beefsteak fruits. They are round, smooth and very meaty, with few seeds and a mild flavor. OP. 77 days.

Ace 55 VFA

One of the 'Ace' series, all strong-growing determinates that need a stake, trellis or cage. All are adapted to the southwest and other places with hot, dry summers. Large red fruits have good flavor and color. 'Ace' and 'Ace 55' are so low in acid, they should not be used for canning. OP. 80 days.

Beefmaster VFN

A Petoseed release formerly known as 'Beefeater' produces red fruit as large as

38

One of the highest-rated tomatoes for yield and flavor, 'Better Boy' needs strong stakes or trellising and a long season of warm weather.

2 pounds. Park's 1996 catalog says the vigorous indeterminate bears "unbelievable quantities." H. 73 to 80 days.

Better Boy VFN

A vigorous indeterminate with good disease resistance and a continuous yield of large, smooth, high-quality red tomatoes that average 10 to 16 ounces. The plants need staking or trellising. A good leaf cover helps prevent sunscald in southern gardens. "One of the best-tasting, best-producing garden tomatoes available anywhere," the Tomato Growers Supply Company says. In taste tests at the Alabama Agricultural Experiment Station, this one, along with 'Monte Carlo,' rated highest. H. 78 days.

Big Beef VFFNTSA

An All-America winner in 1994, 'Big Beef' has the decided advantage of almost total disease resistance, including tolerance to diseases not listed above. Smooth, thin-skinned red fruit averages 10 to 12 ounces and is borne on indeterminate vines in greater quantities than found on most large-fruited varieties. Vesey's says, "'Big Beef' may be the finest tomato ever developed for the home gardener." Bob Ambrose, publisher of *The Tomato Club* newsletter, puts the admiring sentiment in rhyme: "For those who ponder in great disbelief, the time is ripe to indulge in 'Big Beef!'" H. 73 days.

Big Boy (Burpee's Big Boy)

Twenty years ago, this was the top choice of home gardeners. Now, lack of disease resistance is a handicap, but 'Big Boy' still has fans because of its large, smooth, scarlet, meaty fruit, most a pound or more. "Fruits are smooth, firm and thick-walled, with bright red, meaty flesh of delicious flavor and superb quality," writes Jung. The heavy crops peak in midseason, but indeterminate plants continue to bear a few fruit till frost. H. 78 to 80 days.

Big Girl VF (Burpee's Big Girl)

'Big Girl' is much like 'Big Boy,' but with better disease resistance and slightly smaller fruit. Hybrid indeterminate vines yield firm, solid red fruits as heavy as a pound. "Luscious flavor, no green shoulders and just right for slicing," writes the Tomato Growers Supply Company. H. 78 days.

Brandywine

This Amish heirloom, first recorded in 1885, is known for distinctive color and flavor. "Strong flavor is really brandylike in its intensity and richness," says Bountiful Gardens. "We have not tasted better," says Johnny's. The indeterminate vine produces potatolike foliage and a relatively small number of purplish beefsteak-type fruits weighing from 10 ounces to more than a pound. The fruit is rough in shape and deeply lobed. OP. 74 to 80 days.

Burpee's Supersteak VFN

A long-season indeterminate introduced in 1980, "this is the modern version of the old-fashioned beefsteak, with the imperfections removed," says the Tomato Growers Supply Company. "The fruit has the same rich flavor but slightly more acid and is smoother and less prone to catfacing, with a smaller core and blossom-end scar. Average weight is 1 pound, but they often grow to 2 pounds." H. 80 days.

Cal-Ace VF

An 'Ace' type with improved disease resistance, this favorite of California

gardeners has strong determinate vines that should be staked, trellised or caged. The large red fruit is firm and smooth. OP. 80 days.

Delicious (Burpee's Delicious)

This is the current record holder in the Miracle-Gro giant tomato contest described on page 23. Gordon Graham grew a 7-pound 12-ounce behemoth, but most home gardeners can expect 2-to-3-pound fruit. The flesh is tasty, red and unusually meaty, with small seed cavities. The plant is a strong-growing indeterminate. OP. 77 days.

Dinner Plate

An indeterminate heirloom with red, heart-shaped fruit weighing about 1½ pounds. The flavor is judged excellent by *The Tomato Club* newsletter. The Tomato Growers Supply Company agrees: "Heavy bearer and a superior slicing tomato." OP. 90 to 100 days.

German Johnson

An old-time favorite indeterminate from North Carolina and Virginia, 'German Johnson' is one of the parents of the better-known 'Mortgage Lifter' and has a similar taste. The large, irregularly shaped pink tomatoes average 1 pound and are meaty with few seeds, so they are good for slicing, sauces or canning. OP. 80 to 90 days.

Giant Belgium

This indeterminate heirloom, which hails not from Europe but from Ohio, produces a relatively small number of solid, deep pink fruits, much like 'Brandywine,' but as large as 5 pounds. Jeanette Crumper of Dallas wrote in *The Tomato Club* newsletter that she considers the flavor better than that of the similar 'Pink Ponderosa,' 'Dutchman,' 'Oxheart,' 'Brandywine' and 'Wa-

Many of the largest tomatoes are heirlooms, such as the Amish 'Brandywine' (first recorded in 1885), whose seeds have been saved for generations.

termelon Pink.' However, 'Giant Belgium' is susceptible to cracking and fungal diseases. OP. 85 to 90 days.

Giant Oxheart (Oxheart)

According to Southern Exposure, the oxheart shape, rounded with a pointed tip, is the result of a single gene mutation around 1925. Indeterminate vines bear very meaty, thick-walled, mild-flavored pink fruit weighing 1 or 2 pounds. Plants should be supported in cages to help protect the fruit from sunscald. OP. 80 to 88 days.

Golden Boy A

The first hybrid yellow tomato ever developed, 'Golden Boy' is later to mature than some more recent releases, but yields are good and the mild flavor is pleasant. Fruit is large, round and deep golden. The vigorous indeterminate plants need staking. H. 75 to 80 days.

Hy-Beef 9904 VFT

This Stokes release is unusual because the red jumbo beefsteak fruit, as heavy as 14 ounces, has the consistency of a paste tomato, 20 percent more dense than a normal globe-shaped tomato. The fruit is semi-seedless and recommended for fresh eating, sauces or sun drying. "Great taste!" says Stokes. Because of its meatiness, it is resistant to cracking and will keep at least 10 days after ripe picking. The bushy determinate plants need staking. H. 70 days.

Jubilee ACS (Golden Jubilee)

This old-timer developed by the Burpee Seed Company has bright golden yellow, medium-to-large fruits on vigorous indeterminate plants that require staking. 'Jubilee' has a distinctively sweet,

'Principe Borghese' is an heirloom paste tomato whose fruits are so meaty that they are grown in Italy just for drying outdoors in the sun.

mild flavor, though it is not low in acid. OP. 80 to 83 days.

Mortgage Lifter (Radiator Charlie's)
According to Southern Exposure, both unusual names came from its West Virginian creator, Radiator Charlie, who sold plants for $1 each in the 1940s and paid the $6,000 mortgage on his house in 6 years. (Radiator Charlie's own unusual name came from his other business, repairing radiators). The indeterminate heirloom is meaty with few seeds, similar to 'Giant Belgium' but a bit smaller. OP. 79 to 85 days.

Nepal
This 12-ounce red beefsteak tomato is said to have originated in the Himalayas. "A high-quality intense tomato flavor," says the Tomato Growers Supply Company. Indeterminate plants bear well even in cooler weather, and fruit matures early for its size. OP. 78 days.

Ponderosa (Beefsteak, Pink Ponderosa)
An old-timer with very large, flattened, thick-walled, pink, green-shouldered, meaty fruits with excellent flavor and small seed cavities. The large, indeterminate plants should be staked or trellised. It has no known disease resistance, so yields may be small. Slow to mature, it should be grown only in long-season areas. Grow it in cages to protect the fruit from sunscald. OP. 80 days.

Shady Lady VFNSA
Named for a unique growth habit, with sturdy, upright vines and large leaves that protect the fruit from sunscald, this determinate is a good choice for hot, sunny places, where other tomatoes suffer. The smooth, red globe fruit is

firm and resistant to cracking and blotching. H. 75 days.

Supersteak

"Tomatoes as big as grapefruits," Thompson & Morgan says. Among the earliest of the beefsteaks, with smooth, uniformly round and delicious fruits. Indeterminate plants are vigorous and disease-resistant. H. 80 days.

Top Sirloin VFNT

New in 1997, with 12-ounce red beefsteak fruit that is smooth around the shoulders, with little catfacing and a small blossom scar. The crack-resistant fruits ripen from the inside out. Indeterminate plants have multiple disease resistance "One of the earliest we've seen for a variety so big-fruited, so luscious," Ferry-Morse writes. H. 75 days.

Ultra Boy VFN

A large-fruited member of Stokes' 'Ultra' series, this indeterminate has good-tasting red fruit, at least a pound apiece. "In our opinion, certainly the best of the extra-large-fruited 'Boy' series," says Stokes. The fruit is 4 or 5 days earlier than 'Better Boy,' 'Wonder Boy' and 'Supersonic.' It also has "good keeping quality," says the Tomato Growers Supply Company. H. 72 days.

Whopper Improved VFFNT

In 1996, Park introduced an improved version of its top-selling indeterminate, earlier with better disease resistance. Round, red fruits grow big till season's end. H. 65 days.

Yellow Oxheart

A family heirloom from Virginia, this 1-pound, yellow, oxheart-shaped tomato is rated superb in every way except disease resistance and tolerance to drought. Also, seedling vigor is poor.

Southern Exposure writes: "Rates in the top 5 percent of all yellow and golden tomatoes in our trials and was the top performer in its class at every trial location in the mid-Atlantic and Northeast. The sweet fruits have a small core and a distinctive rich, full and exceptionally well-balanced flavor." Indeterminate. OP. 79 days.

PASTE TOMATOES

Amish Paste

This Amish heirloom has indeterminate vines that bear oblong, 8-ounce, ox-heart-shaped paste tomatoes, "solid, with an outstandingly good, sweet flavor," says the Tomato Growers Supply Company. OP. 85 days.

Artela

A semi-determinate vine that bears a large crop of meaty fruit in a short time, "which makes it possible to cook up a big batch of sauce all at once," says The Cook's Garden. H. 70 days.

Aztec VFN

Tolerance to VFN as well as bacterial speck and alternaria in a bright red-fruited determinate. H. 68 days.

Banana Legs

This unusual tomato, 4 inches long and 1½ inches wide, is dry enough to be well suited to making pastes or sauces. Most fruits are solid yellow, but some have light green stripes. The determinate plant has lacy foliage. OP. 75 to 90 days.

Bellestar (Bellstar)

A determinate with larger-than-usual fruit, at 4 to 6 ounces, this Canadian release is meaty and dark red. No disease tolerance, but fruit is crack-resistant. Johnny's says, "The best mid-early

'Roma' is a classic paste tomato: pear- or plum-shaped, with thick red flesh.

processor for roadside stands and home gardens." OP. 65 to 70 days.

Heinz 1350 VF
This hybrid was released in 1963 for canning, but the 6-to-8-ounce crack-resistant fruits can also be eaten fresh. Bright red fruit is borne heavily on determinate plants. Ripening is fairly uniform, which allows for picking one large harvest. OP. 70 to 75 days.

Italian Gold VF
New in 1997, this variety has unusual gold, pear-shaped fruit. Compact, determinate plants are disease-resistant. Petoseed recommends that this "prolific yielder" be grown in cages or tied to short stakes. H. 75 days.

LaRoma VF
A determinate with uniform, 3-to-4-ounce fruit. "Produces seven times more fruit than the standard 'Roma' in field trials," says the Tomato Growers Supply Company. H. 62 days.

La Rossa VFF
"The best paste tomato in our trials," said Park Seeds in 1996. Johnny's adds, "While not suitable for salad use, in our kitchen tests, 'La Rossa' made thick, fresh-tasting tomato sauce much faster than other processing tomatoes" because of its small seed cavity. 'La Rossa' is a determinate whose red, meaty, pear-shaped fruits weigh about 4 ounces. H. 75 to 78 days.

Principe Borghese
This heirloom is grown in Italy just for drying. Determinate plants hold the clusters of small fruit so well, says The Cook's Garden, "that gardeners in arid climates can sun-dry whole plants." In its Kentucky trials of open-pollinated

tomatoes, *HortIdeas* magazine noted, "Severe early-blight symptoms but still very productive, with good taste, and keeps well on the vine a long time." OP. 65 to 75 days.

Roma VF
Plum-shaped, medium-to-small red fruits developed by the Harris Seed Company have good color and solids for processing. The tough skin is easy to peel. Strong, determinate plants can be allowed to sprawl on mulch. Yields are heavy. OP. 75 to 78 days.

San Marzano
Larger and later than some others, with 3-inch-long, deep red, almost rectangular fruit on indeterminate vines. Its small, distinct seed cavity can be scooped out, leaving all meat for faster cooking into paste. The Cook's Garden recommends this variety for drying. OP. 75 to 80 days.

Super Marzano VFNT
Indeterminate vines bear pear-shaped fruit that averages 5 inches long. The fruit is high in pectin, so produces a naturally thick sauce. Plants are tall and resistant to bacterial speck. H. 70 days.

Veeroma VF
A small determinate plant whose fruit is better-yielding and more crack-resistant than that of 'Roma.' OP. 72 days.

Viva Italia VFFNA
William Dam assures us that this tomato is nicknamed "the Italian stallion. This variety is really a winner in your garden by many lengths." A determinate whose pear-shaped fruits have a higher sugar content than many others, 'Viva Italia' is also suitable for fresh eating. Vesey's writes: "Do not be fooled later in the season when the fruits are still green.

'San Marzano's' small, distinct seed cavity is easy to scoop out.

'Viva Italia' ripens from the inside out rather than from the bottom up." Very disease-resistant and sets fruit better in hot weather than does the original 'Roma.' H. 75 to 80 days.

UNUSUAL TOMATOES

Angora
Softly furry leaves and stems distinguish this indeterminate, whose fruits are medium-size, bright red, smooth and solid, with a mild flavor. The Tomato Growers Supply Company notes that an occasional seed will not come true to type, so seedlings without fuzzy stems and leaves should be discarded. OP. 68 days.

Big Rainbow
This 2-pound indeterminate heirloom is "the most visually spectacular we have grown," says Southern Exposure. "As fruits ripen, they resemble a rainbow: green on the shoulder, yellow in the middle and red on the blossom end. When fully ripe, the fruits are gold on the stem end and red on the blossom   45

end." The Cook's Garden comments, "They are subject to cracks and catfacing, but what a treat to eat. Sliced, they are a thing of beauty and great for sandwiches or for eating with just a topping of shredded fresh basil so that you can appreciate their superb flavor." OP. 80 to 90 days.

Black Krim

Not exactly black, but a dark brown-red that turns darker in hot weather, when this heirloom tomato excels. The fruit is 10 to 12 ounces and prone to cracking, but the indeterminate vines produce heavy crops. Bountiful Gardens says, "One of those luscious gourmet types that are terrible shippers. So juicy and has such a delicate skin that it's a problem just to get it off the vine and into the house, but well worth the effort. Unfortunately, also a favorite with night-marauding rodents in our garden." OP. 75 to 90 days.

Burgess Stuffing

This red tomato is hollow inside, like a pepper, and thus ideal for stuffing. The firm fruits are a little wider than 3 inches. The plants are determinate. OP. 78 days.

Cherokee Purple

This Tennessee heirloom, dating from before 1890, reportedly comes from the Cherokee tribe, who developed very productive, short indeterminate plants that bear potatolike foliage and dusky rose-purple, green-shouldered, 10-to-12-ounce fruits with brick-red flesh and green gel. "The tomatoes are absolutely delicious, with a pleasantly sweet and rich flavor," says the Tomato Growers Supply Company. "With thin skin and soft flesh, the fruit is somewhat perishable, but they taste so good, they will be eaten quickly anyhow." OP. 80 days.

Currant Tomato (German Raisin)

This is the only tomato you will likely grow that is not a member of the species *Lycopersicum esculentum*. It is a cousin, *L. pimpinellifolium*. Fruits, which are borne in great abundance in trusses on indeterminate vines, are only about half an inch across. They are tasty but very susceptible to cracking. There are both red and yellow types: 'Red Currant,' 'Yellow Currant' and 'Gold Currant.' Johnny's writes, "The species is naturally resistant to many diseases, including fusarium wilt, late blight, bacterial canker, bacterial wilt and spotted wilt virus." OP, though they easily cross with other tomatoes growing nearby. All about 70 days.

Evergreen (Emerald Evergreen)

An heirloom indeterminate whose beefsteak fruit is green with yellow stripes

Gardeners who grow tomatoes from seed have the best choice of color, including the small yellow 'Cherry Gold' and the larger golden 'Persimmon.'

when ripe. The flavor is much like that of a red tomato. "This is one of the best tomatoes we know of that's green when ripe. Mild, delicious flavor," says the Tomato Growers Supply Company. These plants stand up well in hot, humid weather. OP. 70 to 72 days.

Great White

"There are a number of heirloom 'white' tomatoes, and this looks like the best one," says Johnny's. With tomatoes larger than those of 'White Beauty' and a color "reminiscent of fresh pineapple,"

'Great White' was introduced by Ohio seedsman George Gleckler in the late 1970s, when he found an unusual pale yellow beefsteak in a crop of 'Orange Oxheart.' The flavor is sweet and mild. Vigorous indeterminate plants have heavy foliage that protects the fruit from sunscald. OP. 85 days.

Green Grape

One-inch fruit of very good flavor grows in clusters on a short, compact determinate plant. The color when ripe is green with yellow highlights, similar to

47

the beefsteak 'Evergreen.' "Its flavor is easily in the top 5 percent of the varieties we have grown," Southern Exposure says. OP. 70 days.

Long Keeper

This big orange semi-determinate tomato is famous for its keeping qualities. Picked when it has a pale pink blush and stored unwrapped at 60 to 70 degrees F, unblemished fruit can last through the winter without a change in flavor or texture. "Though the quality doesn't match that of a fresh garden tomato, flavor and texture is superior to most winter supermarket tomatoes," says Southern Exposure. OP. 78 days.

Micro-Tom

Advertised as "the world's smallest tomato," this 1990 release from the University of Florida bears 1-inch red fruit on a determinate plant only 5 to 8 inches tall, perfect for small, 4-inch pots on a windowsill. H. 85 days from seed.

Persimmon

This American heirloom produces large, 12-ounce-to-2-pound golden beefsteak fruits on indeterminate vines. "Ripens from the blossom end to the softly dented light green shoulders, gradually acquiring a rose-orange hue," writes Southern Exposure. The Cook's Garden adds, "The deep oblate fruits really do look just like ripe persimmons, and the taste is out of this world." Territorial Seeds calls it "by far the most flavorful yellow tomato we have ever trialed." OP. 80 days.

Pineapple

Bicolored red-and-yellow fruit as heavy as 2 pounds, streaked inside and out. "The flavor is wonderful—rich, fruity and sweet," says the Tomato Growers Supply Company. "This heirloom tomato

'Purple Calabash' has big, ruffled fruit.

is a standout in everyone's garden." Indeterminate. OP. 85 days.

Purple Calabash (Red Calabash)

Fruits of this heirloom indeterminate are thin-skinned, very sweet and weigh about ¼ pound. The fruits are ruffled. "An ugly tomato that's truly delicious for those who understand that beauty is not skin-deep," says Seeds of Change, but Gleckler's says, "I must be honest, they are of poor quality, mostly a novelty." OP. 85 days.

Red Pear

Companion to 'Yellow Pear' (page 49), this unusually shaped cherry tomato is perfect in summer salads. Fruit is low-acid. Indeterminate. OP. 70 to 78 days.

Tigerella (Mr. Stripey)

Yellow-orange stripes on a red background distinguish this 1½-to-2-inch tomato. Vines are indeterminate and very productive. In Britain, 'Tigerella' won the Royal Horticultural Society award of merit, says Thompson & Morgan: "Fruits have an appealing tart-sweet flavor, and the coloring adds extra appeal to fresh salads." Also recommended for greenhouses. OP. 56 to 65 days.

Tigerette Cherry
Oval-shaped, striped orange and red fruits grow on dwarf plants that have ornamental yellowish green foliage, an excellent choice for containers in the flowerbed. This is a Stokes exclusive. OP. 68 days.

Watermelon Beefsteak
Watermelon-shaped, oblong and 2 pounds or heavier, this century-old tomato also features unusual pink skin and purplish red flesh. Vines are indeterminate. OP. 75 days.

White Beauty (Snowball)
Creamy white inside and out when ripe, this ½-pound, meaty tomato has a high sugar content and mild flavor. Vines are indeterminate. "Close your eyes. Can you tell it's not red by tasting?" asks Seeds Blüm. "If you are troubled by strong tomato flavor, this is the tomato for you," says Gleckler's. OP. 80 to 85 days.

White Wonder
One of the varieties served in Alice Waters' famous Chez Panisse restaurant, this has the same creamy-colored fruit of 'Great White' and 'White Beauty' but smaller, 4 to 6 ounces. Southern Exposure writes, "We like to serve it as an ingredient in a multicolor tomato marinade (tomatoes, garlic, vinegar, oil, pepper and herbal seasonings)." The indeterminate vines develop less foliage

'Yellow Pear' is pretty and tasty.

than others do, so sunscald can be a problem. OP. 84 days.

Yellow Pear
An heirloom first described in 1805, with small, clear yellow, pear-shaped fruits that are pretty in salads, especially in the company of 'Red Pear.' Indeterminate plants are suitable for containers but should be staked or caged. "Probably the only tomato our kids like better than 'Red Pear,'" writes Shepherd Ogden of The Cook's Garden, and, "A personal favorite of [his wife] Ellen's as well, who loves their mild, almost lemony flavor." OP. 70 to 78 days.

Yellow Stuffer
This unusual fruit looks like a pepper inside and out but is a golden yellow, square, 6-ounce tomato, a companion to 'Burgess Stuffing.' Indeterminate plants must be staked. OP. 76 to 80 days.

The Tomato Ward

Managing Diseases, Pests and Disorders

If gardens were Edens and tomatoes were perfect, there would be no need for this chapter. Alas, an endless silent parade of bugs, slugs, worms, germs, rots, spots and disfigurations comes un-invited into almost every garden. Any of these villains can not only crash the garden party but devastate the fruits of the gardener's labors.

Chapter 2 focused on what tomatoes want. This chapter is the opposite, the flip side of the issue: what tomatoes don't want. If a gardener doesn't give the plants what they want, they will be more prone to diseases and disorders, even pests. Not that the situation is entirely under the gardener's control. The weather plays a big part. Tomatoes need plenty of light and warmth, preferably in the temperature range of 60 to 85 degrees F. You can't choose your neighborhood, either, and you have to accept certain limitations of soil and air quality. However, if you can manage to give your plants reasonably fertile soil, well drained and high in organic matter, a consistent supply of clean, air-temperature water and steady, minimal feeding without overfeeding, you will help the plants immeasurably. Inspect the garden once a day or as often as you can so that if problems do arise, you can nip them in the bud. And when it comes to disease resistance, take advantage of the ace that plant breeders have tucked up your sleeve. Many tomato varieties have inbred defenses against disease, a feature that can make the difference between a big, healthy crop and a small, poor one or none at all.

The remainder of this chapter describes not only tomato diseases but some additional problems that might beset your little green charges as they make their perilous way from tender seedlings to towers of ripening fruit and lush, healthy foliage. Diagnosis can be tricky. Nutritional disorders resemble certain diseases, and the diseases themselves are difficult to label unless you have a scientific photo guide in front of you. Don't do anything drastic in terms of sprays or corrective fertilizers until you have the blessing of an expert—you might worsen the situation and could do long-term damage to your soil. Safe measures you can take to minimize problems and promote plant health are always available—just go back to Chapter 2 and figure out what the plants want. At the end of the season, dispose of diseased plants not by composting them but by putting them in the garbage or burying them in a hole a couple of feet deep.

DISEASES

Just as there are different types of human diseases, there are several general classes of plant diseases: those caused by bacteria, fungi and viruses. To minimize disease outbreaks, look for tomato varieties resistant to diseases in your area. Keep the tomato bed clean of old plant material, rotate it to a new spot every year—preferably not a place used last year for potatoes, eggplants or peppers—and do not overfeed with nitrogen, which can worsen many diseases and disorders. A description of the most common follows.

Bacterial Diseases

Tomatoes totally resistant to bacterial diseases have not yet been developed, though it is always a good practice to grow more than one variety to take advantage of subtle differences in disease tolerance.

Bacterial wilt is a problem in the trop-

ics and into the southern states. Farther north, bacterial spot and canker infect leaves and stems.

Bacterial speck, which causes black spots or lesions to form on fruit, flowers and leaves, has recently become a serious problem for northern growers. If conditions are favorably humid, these bacteria multiply rapidly, oozing out through the leaves and broken stems. Dry weather and fertile soil lessen bacterial problems.

Fungal Diseases

Fungal diseases are probably responsible for most of the specking and spotting of the fruits, as well as the spotting, wilting and blackening of the foliage and stems of your tomatoes. Fortunately, some tomatoes have a decided resistance or tolerance to certain fungal diseases, but there are also cultural techniques that make a critical difference. All fungal diseases spread on wet plants. Try not to wet the leaves during watering—water the ground only—and do not work among wet plants. Do not overfertilize or overwater. Should a disease outbreak occur, try one of several fungicides on the market. The most benign, favored by organic growers, are those containing copper. A homemade spray made from one teaspoon baking soda (sodium bicarbonate) in a quart of water also helps control fungal diseases. Spraying can be stopped during dry weather in summer but should be resumed before the onset of fall rains. Some gardeners find that garlic sprays also help prevent fungus outbreaks. Mulched plots have fewer fungus problems, because mulches prevent soil-borne fungi from splashing onto the lower leaves.

EARLY BLIGHT (Alternaria solani): All early, high-yielding determinates are susceptible to early blight. The most damaging disease of tomatoes grown east of the Mississippi is aggravated by hot days, humid nights and heavy dews. The fungus overwinters in the soil and usually infects plants when it is splashed onto foliage during rain or watering. The oldest leaves are infected first, showing brown or black, round or angular spots with concentric rings, so-called target spots. The spotted leaves may die and drop prematurely. Fruit may develop dark, leathery decayed spots, especially at the stem end. Recently developed resistant varieties carry the initial A (or AS, for alternaria stem canker) after their names. Although older varieties are not given the same initials, some evidence exists that heirloom types with potatolike foliage have tolerance or resistance as well. Growing resistant or tolerant varieties is probably a better defense than using fungicides. In experiments in Simcoe, Ontario, no significant difference in production was apparent between plants sprayed with fungicide and those not sprayed, but resistant tomatoes such as 'Celebrity,' 'Mountain Pride' and 'Sunny' were least infected. The use of mulches that prevent splashing of infected soil onto plants has also proved effective.

ANTHRACNOSE (Colletotrichum coccodes): This disease causes sunken, circular spots to develop rapidly on ripe fruit late in the season—after mid-September in the north. It is most prevalent on tomatoes grown in sandy soils, and there is little cultivar resistance. Use mulch, rotate crops, and support plants upright to help prevent infection from the soil.

DAMPING OFF: An umbrella name that covers several soilborne fungi, this disease affects seedlings grown in unsterilized soil. The tiny stems become pinched at or below the soil level and eventually topple over and die. Use sterilized soil or a purchased seedling mix to start seeds. If you notice damping off at one end of a seedling flat, remove the healthy seedlings to sterilized soil as soon as possible. A soil drench of a solution of one teaspoon baking soda (sodium bicarbonate) in one quart of room-temperature water will help control the spread of the disease.

FUSARIUM WILT (Fusarium spp): The symptoms of fusarium and verticillium wilt are almost identical, but fusarium is more common in the south. Fusarium wilt was one of the first diseases successfully tackled by plant breeders. In the late 1940s and early '50s, the first fusarium-resistant tomatoes, 'Homestead' and 'Marglobe Supreme,' were released. Tomatoes with inbred resistance are marked with the initial F after the cultivar name. The usual symptoms of fusarium wilt are wilting of leaves on one side of the plant, progressing upward from the base, or of leaflets on one side of the leaf. Leaves often turn yellow before they die. New strains of fusarium wilt have shown up in tomato growing regions of California and Florida. Plants with resistance to the earlier strains are not necessarily resistant to the later types. The tomato listings in Chapter 3 identify tomatoes with known resistance to later strains. Cool weather restricts the development of fusarium wilt.

GRAY MOLD (Botrytis spp): This is a common cause of fruit rot. It may appear as stem rot or as spots on fruit. Fungal spores often enter wounds caused by pests or by physiological problems such as cracking or catfacing.

LATE BLIGHT (Phytophthora infestans): Best known as the disease that led to the Irish Potato Famine in the mid-1800s, late blight can be devastating to tomatoes as well. During the 1990s, a new strain of the fungus has been wiping out entire crops in North America. The disease can spread from potatoes to tomatoes and vice versa. The first symptoms on either vegetable, usually seen after a period of wet weather, are blackened shoots, dark lesions on stems and water-soaked or black, greasy-looking areas on the leaves. In the morning, look on the underside of a leaf for a ring of shiny white spores surrounding the infected part. Fruit will also be affected if wet weather continues after the disease appears. Tomato fruit rot may be slow but will destroy the fruit before it ripens, turning it into inedible mush. Infected green fruits harvested in fall turn black in storage. If you see any symptoms of late blight, pull up and destroy the plants and send them to a dump or bury them in a deep hole.

Late blight can spread only when plants are wet. Water the ground, not the foliage. Where summers are rainy, plant tomatoes against a south-facing

Tomato Rot

This troublesome disease often causes much loss to the tomato crop. Last season, when the tomatoes had grown to the size of hickory nuts, the plants were given a thorough spraying with Bordeaux mixture. Three weeks later, the application was repeated. Very little rot was found on the plants sprayed, while on plants purposely left untreated, many diseased fruits were noticed. The season being a remarkably dry one, the rot did not do the usual amount of damage to the crop. The results seem to show conclusively that the disease can be kept in check by the use of Bordeaux if treatment is begun early in the season.

—*Twenty-Fourth Annual Report of the Secretary of the State Horticultural Society of Michigan, 1894*

(Editor's note: Bordeaux consists of copper sulfate, lime and water. One early encyclopedia specifies 14 pounds, 9½ pounds and 100 gallons, respectively.)

wall, where they can be protected from the rain by the overhanging eaves or a temporary lean-to. In the open, tomatoes can be sheltered under polyethylene held at least a foot above the plants. Coastal gardeners report that seaweed mulch lessens late-blight infections.

Late blight can overwinter in the soil only if it is frost-free. In the north, it survives in potato seed and can be blown into the garden from diseased tomatoes or potatoes growing nearby.

SOUTHERN BLIGHT (Sclerotium rolfsii): The most troublesome fungal disease of North American tomatoes where temperatures and humidity are high, southern blight is seldom seen in places with cold winters. The first symptom is a severe wilting. At the soil line, the stem becomes brown and soft and covered with cottony mold. Southern blight lives in the soil, where it may persist for years.

VERTICILLIUM WILT (Verticillium spp): The symptoms of fusarium and verticillium wilt are almost identical, but verticillium is more common in the north. One of the most common and destructive diseases for commercial growers of tomatoes, eggplants, potatoes and cotton, especially in the cool climates, this soil-borne fungus causes leaves to turn yellow, dry up and die progressively from the base of the plant to the top. Plants may survive the season, but they will be stunted and their fruit will be undersized. Eventually, the only leaves remaining will be those on the branch tips, and even they will tend to curl upward, so fruit remaining late in the season is often damaged by sunscald. The initial V after the cultivar name indicates inbred resistance.

VIRUSES

Several viruses can infect tomatoes. Most of these microscopic organisms survive in the plants themselves, sometimes even in their seeds, and in related weeds such as nightshades. Infection can be spread by the use of infected pruning tools, but the usual culprits are insects that pierce the vegetable skin. So while small sucking pests such as aphids, whiteflies, thrips and leafhoppers may do little damage in terms of what they consume, they pose a greater danger as disease agents. For this reason, tomatoes should not be planted near beets or spinach in places such as Colorado, where beet leafhoppers are common. Infected plants should be removed and put in the garbage.

CUCUMBER MOSAIC VIRUS (CMV): Tomato leaves become distinctly narrow—called the "shoestring" symptom—and may resemble leaves damaged by exposure to the herbicide 2,4-D. Plants become stunted and may develop no full-size fruit.

TOBACCO MOSAIC VIRUS (TMV): Mosaic viruses are named for their chief symptom: a mosaiclike yellow mottling of the foliage. Tobacco mosaic virus is the most infectious of all plant viruses. It is also extremely durable, capable of withstanding heat and existing for many years even when dry. Infected leaves often look crinkled or have curled edges, sometimes thin and fernlike. Infected fruits may reveal internal browning and gray or brown walls when cut open. Varieties with inbred resistance have the initials T or TMV after their name. In experiments in Canada, spraying plants with milk was shown to limit the spread of TMV.

TOMATO SPOTTED WILT VIRUS (TSWV): Called "the AIDS virus of greenhouse plants" by *HortIdeas* magazine, TSWV is spreading rapidly and has no cure. The disease is spread from plant to plant mainly by western flower thrips. More than 100 plant species are vulnerable. Symptoms include wilting and death of growing tips, as well as half-inch-wide spots with concentric rings on fruits. Greenhouse operators use sticky blue cards to monitor thrip populations and check new plants susceptible to TSWV for infection before they are brought into the greenhouse.

NUTRITIONAL DISORDERS

Nutritional disorders caused by a shortage or overabundance of certain minerals in the soil can be difficult to treat without upsetting the soil balance. For

55

healthiest growth, tomatoes need soil that is slightly acidic or about neutral. Provided the temperature is in the tomato's "comfort range" and conditions are neither too wet nor too dry, nutrients in the soil will be available to the plant roots. Too acidic or alkaline, too hot or cold, too wet or dry, and certain nutrient imbalances will result. A mild organic fertilizer such as compost or a fertilizer specified for tomatoes can help to minimize problems. But beware: Too much fertilizer is an invitation to nutritional disorders.

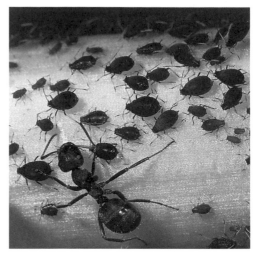

Aphids suck sap and spread diseases.

PESTS

APHID: Aphids of many colors are common pests outdoors but usually pose no serious problem. Indoors, populations of these small, soft-bodied pests can build to such levels that their sap sucking weakens plants. Both indoors and out, they act as disease vectors, especially for viruses. In small numbers, they can be knocked off plants or squashed by hand. Larger populations can be killed with insecticidal-soap spray. Encourage lady beetles in the garden, because they eat aphids.

COLORADO POTATO BEETLE: Given the choice, this yellow, black-striped beetle and its orange or brown, spotted larvae will eat potatoes, not tomatoes. Gardeners who grow a lot of tomatoes sometimes cultivate an outer row of potatoes as a trap crop. In any case, these pests are large and easily hand-picked or knocked into a jar of soapy water. Rotenone or pyrethrum sprays will also kill them.

CUTWORM: There are several types of cutworm, all larvae of night-flying moths. These larvae are brownish or grayish and about an inch long. One type severs plant stems shortly after they have been transplanted into the garden. Any sort of collar that extends at least an inch into and above the ground will provide protection. Surround individual plants with tin cans, both ends removed, or with pieces of cardboard tubing. When damage does occur, usually overnight, dig into the soil around the damaged stem the next morning. Often you will uncover the culprit nearby, just under the soil surface. Variegated cutworms lay their eggs throughout tomato foliage in summer, and the young larvae feed on the fruit, boring holes into it and paving the way for rot problems.

FLEA BEETLE: These tiny black hardshelled beetles that jump when disturbed are most troublesome on young plants early in the season, when growth is slow and the soil is cool. Plants that grow rapidly can outpace the damage, which appears as peppery holes. Rotenone will kill flea beetles but is seldom justified.

NEMATODES: Many species of these roundworms exist, some beneficial and

The Colorado potato beetle larva prefers potatoes but sometimes grazes tomatoes.

some invisible to the naked eye. Some nematodes eat roots and therefore damage plants unseen, causing wilting and slowed growth. Tomato varieties resistant to the most troublesome nematodes are marked with the initial N after the cultivar name. The type of nematode that the N tomatoes resist is most prevalent in coarse-textured, sandy soils in California and other areas of the south. This species seldom if ever overwinters in the northern states and Canada, though it can be a greenhouse pest. Certain types of marigolds, such as the Gem series, produce root exudates that repel nematodes. Planting these marigolds around tomatoes or growing marigolds in the tomato patch a year ahead will help clean out the soil.

SLUG: In damp weather, this soft-bodied pest may eat tomato fruit. Characteristic damage is a slimy trail on the fruit ending in a pit through the skin. Make sure tomato fruit is supported above the ground, encourage good air circulation through plants by planting sufficiently far apart, and pick ripe fruit regularly.

SPIDER MITE: The first sign that a colony of these minute, sap-sucking pests are at work is yellowing and curling leaves that, when inspected, reveal a network of fine webbing. Spider mites are most problematic in hot, dry weather and on plants grown indoors. Spray with insecticidal soap.

STINKBUG: This shield-shaped bug about half an inch long is named for the foul odor it releases if squashed. It feeds by sticking its mouthparts into the fruit, leaving white or yellow blemishes in its wake. Insecticidal soap or rotenone will kill stinkbugs, but they are usually too few and far apart to be worth spraying. 57

Cutworms often feed at night.

They are most troublesome in gardens grown near grassy fields or weedy areas, where the bugs spend most of the year.

TOMATO FRUITWORM (Corn earworm): This hairless caterpillar is about 1½ inches long and may be green, brown or pink. It eats holes in fruit but seldom foliage. Natural compounds in petunia leaves have been shown to repel them, so it is possible that a spray made from petunia leaves could act as a natural repellent. *Bacillus thuringiensis* (Bt) spray will kill them.

TOMATO HORNWORM: Also known as tobacco hornworm, this sphinx moth larva can become as big as your index finger. Droppings that appear on leaves and under plants are black and easily visible. Damage appears as large bites chewed out of fruit and leaves stripped from plants. Hornworms are mostly easily handpicked or knocked into a pail of soapy water. *Bacillus thuringiensis* (Bt) also kills them. Hornworms bearing white egg cases should not be destroyed, because these are the eggs of parasitic wasps that will hatch and kill additional hornworms.

WHITEFLY: In the north, whitefly is largely a problem of plants grown indoors, where infestations can be fairly easily monitored with sticky yellow boards and combated with insecticidal soap or an alcohol spray.

In Florida, silverleaf whitefly, formerly known as sweet potato whitefly, is a serious problem for outdoor tomatoes. The tiny flies, which form a cloud like ashes when disturbed, suck out stem juices, causing mottling and weakening of plants; but more important, they are vectors for plant viruses. In trials at the University of Florida, either pyrethroid insecticide or Sunspray oil, made by Safer, effectively repelled whiteflies for several days.

PHYSIOLOGICAL DISORDERS

These are not diseases but physical problems caused by less-than-perfect temperatures, soil-nutrient, light or water levels or handling procedures. Most physiological disorders are related to the weather and thus vary from year to year even in the same cultivar grown in the same garden. But another important factor is that certain cultivars are more prone or resistant to disorders than are others. This information often appears in variety descriptions in catalogs or on seed packets.

BLOSSOM-END ROT (BER) AND BLACKHEART: Dramatic and ugly, BER is a hard, sunken, dark area on the bottom, or blossom end, of a tomato. Its internal equivalent,

Stinkbugs pierce fruit skin, leaving hard white or yellow blemishes behind.

which may not be apparent on the skin, is descriptively called blackheart. Both disorders are initiated by water stress, which hampers calcium uptake. Just half an hour of water stress with very slight visible wilting can initiate cell breakdown in the blossom end of the fruit, especially when the fruit is about half-grown. BER is most common and serious when moisture conditions fluctuate, so it is often seen on plants grown in sandy, salty or poor soils with low water-holding capacity and low organic matter. Overzealous gardeners tilling between rows can damage enough roots to cause BER. Interestingly, high humidity during the day can also inhibit calcium transport to tomato fruit, contributing to BER problems. Overfertilization with nitrogen can be an added factor. If your plants have had blossom-end rot in the past, water regularly during dry periods, mulch plants to even out the water supply and add gypsum at planting time at a rate of 5 to 15 pounds per 100 feet of row. Blossom-end rot often shows up on only the first fruit, which should be removed so that the plant can concentrate its energy on later, healthy fruit.

BLOSSOM DROP: If a tomato plant is under any type of stress, it will drop its blossoms, its most expendable part. Temperatures may be too high or too low, light levels may be too dim—especially for plants grown indoors—watering may be too heavy or too light, or plants may have been overfed, especially with nitrogen. In the north, the most common cause is night temperatures below 58 degrees F, though certain cultivars will hold their blossoms when temperatures are considerably lower. In the south, night temperatures above 75 degrees have the same effect.

Curiously, many tomato varieties that set fruit well with cold temperatures will also set well when the weather is hot and thus are resistant to blossom drop in the north or south.

BLOTCHY RIPENING (graywall): Green and yellow mottled areas on what are supposed to be red tomatoes have many possible causes. Tobacco mosaic virus is the most likely reason, but if you are growing a resistant variety, consider low soil potassium and boron levels, too much nitrogen fertilizer, low sunlight or damage by sucking insects such as stinkbugs. Sudden changes in growing conditions, including water stress and chilling injury, can have the same result. In mild cases, ripening may occur but much slower than usual; in severe cases, large, distinct patches remain hard and green even when the rest of the tomato is soft and red. When the fruit is cut, it has a whitish or greenish wall and sometimes brown spots of dead tissue.

CATFACING: Rough tomatoes with protuberances, indentations, scabs and scaly dark green or brown scar tissue on the blossom end (bottom) are usually the result of cool weather during the early stages of fruit formation. At least one week of daytime temperatures of 60 to 65 degrees F and night temperatures of 50 to 60 degrees cause the most severe catfacing; oddly enough, cooler temperatures of 40 to 45 degrees are less damaging, perhaps because growth stops entirely. The first fruits of the season are usually the most affected, though cool weather later in the season can damage later harvests. Exposure to the herbicide 2,4-D can cause similar symptoms.

CHILLING AND FROST INJURY: Tomato fruits are damaged by temperatures under 40 degrees F. The lower the temperature, the drier the weather and the longer the exposure to cold, the more severe the damage will be, as cells continue to collapse and sunken areas form on the skin. Frost causes almost immediate death to exposed areas. Decay will follow unless the fruit is harvested quickly. Chilled tomatoes also lose their ability to ripen properly. When light frost (32 degrees) is forecast, cover plants or pick the fruit; and pick all fruit before a hard frost, one with a temperature under 30 degrees. (See page 19 for information about frost protection.)

CRACKING: Many cultivars are advertised as crack-resistant, but only if they are grown in the areas for which they were developed. For instance, crack-resistant tomatoes selected for dry areas may crack when grown in more humid climates. Severe fluctuations in soil-moisture levels and temperatures can also cause resistant varieties to crack. Certain cultivars are especially prone to this disorder, which often strikes when wet weather follows a period of dry. Consistent watering and mulching to keep water levels constant helps avoid cracking, as does leaving adequate foliage on the plant. Pick susceptible fruit, such as 'Sweet 100,' before it is fully ripe or when rain is forecast.

INTERNAL BROWNING: On the outside, affected tomatoes appear gray, discolored or brown in translucent patches. Inside, there are brown lesions in the wall. Internal browning may be caused by a virus, by water stress or by overfertilization with nitrogen.

LEAF ROLL: This condition, in which leaf edges turn up and inward, is common and seldom a cause for concern, though it is most prevalent on poorly drained soils where plants are staked. Leaf roll is deliberately bred into some early northern cultivars so that the fruit will be exposed to the sun, hastening ripening.

LEATHER-END, ROUGHNESS AND SCARS: These are disorders that begin at the blossom stage. Some cultivars, particularly large-fruited types with green shoulders, suffer from some sort of skin disorder almost every year, while others never do; it is worth searching for tomatoes that suit your own aesthetic standards. Only if fungal spores take advantage of wounds will the fruit be deeply affected. A common cause of these disorders in northern gardens is cool weather, with night temperatures lower than 50 degrees F when the earliest flower clusters are developing. When the weather is cloudy and nights are cool late in the season, thick, leathery skin, bronzed and roughened at the stem end, and patches of hard, green flesh within the ripening fruit may again appear. Too much nitrogen can cause the same damage. Use a high-potash fertilizer, such as wood ashes, and water adequately during periods of drought.

PUFFINESS: Fruit that puffs out in one portion more than another is more common in the greenhouse than in the garden. When the fruit is cut open, a hollow portion is revealed. The usual cause is incomplete pollination, which may be the result of too much nitrogen, too little potassium, too little light, temperatures too high or low, too much wind and drought or ineffective pollination in the greenhouse.

SUNSCALD AND YELLOW-EYE: These two disorders lead to similar yellowing of tomato skin because the development of red pigment has been inhibited. Sunscald may occur whenever ripening fruit, on or off the plant, is exposed to the hot sun for several days. Immature, green fruit is most susceptible. A yellowish white area of sunken tissue appears on the stem end of the fruit or on exposed areas. This may turn blistery and will flatten to a large, grayish white spot with a thin, paperlike skin. Fungus infections often follow. Leaf loss, whether caused by pruning or disease, encourages sunscald, and defoliated plants may require shading with cloth during the hottest parts of the day. Yellow-eye is caused by too much nitrogen fertilizer and water stress. Varieties resistant to verticillium wilt are also resistant to sunscald.

WALNUT WILT: Tomatoes growing within 40 to 50 feet of a black walnut tree or on ground where a black walnut grew within the past three years may wilt and die when they come into contact with a toxin produced by the tree roots.

WHITEWALL (greenback): Hardened and whitened tomato walls that must be cut away before the fruit can be used may be the result of potassium deficiency, water stress or a combination of too little water and too high temperatures. In the greenhouse, the usual cause is low light levels during winter.

POLLUTION INJURY

Sprays and other pollutants in the soil or drifting into your garden can harm or even kill your tomatoes. Some of the most potent agents are aldrin, creosote fumes and the broadleaf herbicides 2,4-D and 2,4,5-T. Gardeners near busy traffic routes, industrial sites or farming areas where chemicals are used should suspect some type of pollution damage if other causes cannot be found for yellowing and wilting of plants.

Pots and Plans

Extending Tomato Space and Time

Tomatoes can be grown in lots of places besides the vegetable garden, and they can be grown earlier or later than the outdoor season would permit. Tomatoes can be picked from a hanging basket, window box or flowerbed. If you use your imagination and concentrate on the seven necessities outlined at the beginning of Chapter 2, you can pick fresh fruit all year, even if you live in an apartment or a desert.

But it won't come quite as easily as the fruit you pick from the garden in summer. An outdoor crop may survive from spring to fall with practically no care, but this will not happen with tomatoes growing in pots or indoors or under any kind of cover. These specialized situations are for the gardener who is either dedicated or desperate. Daily watering and weekly feeding may be required, along with added attention to light levels, temperature, pest and disease control, even pollination.

CONTAINERS OUTDOORS

Tomatoes in pots open new worlds of potential garden spaces: the balcony, the porch, the patio, the rooftop. A tomato in a pot can be moved to follow your one small patch of sun or to hide in the shelter of the garage when frost threatens. Potted tomatoes can be very heavy—a cubic foot of wet soil weighs about 100 pounds—not to mention unwieldy when the fruit starts to swell. So if you want to move a large pot around, look in garden-supply catalogs for pots on wheels or make your own portable setup from scratch or by using a garden cart or a child's wagon.

It is important to match pot size with eventual plant size. Anything can grow in a really big container, but if you want it small, you must choose the tomato carefully. A few varieties that grow less than a foot tall, such as 'Tiny Tim,' 'Toy Boy,' 'Micro-Tom' and 'Red Robin,' will grow in a pot 6 inches across, one plant per pot. The larger cherry tomatoes should be given a pot at least 8 inches wide; with that small amount of soil, you may end up watering twice a day. If you want to grow several plants together, you'll need to increase the pot size. Mimi Luebbermann, author of *Terrific Tomatoes* (Chronicle Books), grows one each of the cherry tomatoes 'Sun Gold,' 'Green Grape' and 'Sweet 100' in a 32-inch-wide plastic container filled with commercial potting mix fortified with a pelleted, low-nitrogen organic fertilizer. To help her with watering, she submerges a tin can, both ends removed, beside each plant and pours water into the cans. This water gradually makes its way to the roots. She mulches with compost when the weather warms up.

If you are growing one of the vigorous indeterminate cherry tomatoes, such as the orange-fruited 'Sun Gold' or the red 'Sweet 100,' remember that the vines grow several feet long. They can be allowed to drape out of a pot that sits on a table, or they can be tied up on a trellis or on strings tied between a porch railing and porch roof. Mimi Luebbermann surrounded her entire container with a ring of wire fencing 5 feet tall. 'Green Grape,' the green-fruited variety that she grew, is a determinate, and so it was the shortest of the three varieties. She wove the stems of all three varieties through the wires as they grew and told *The Tomato Club* newsletter that the result was "a rainbow of salad tomatoes just as ornamental as any basket of petunias."

Although any determinate with medium-to-small fruit is a good choice for

Terra-cotta pots should be lined with plastic to reduce the need for watering.

a pot, several series of tomatoes with medium-size fruit are meant especially for containers. 'Pixie' and 'Patio' are determinates with medium-size fruit. The 'Husky' series are dwarf indeterminates with larger fruit and a fairly stiff central stem. A plant stays neat and tidy within a pot a foot wide, especially if it is given a short cage or 3-foot stake for support as the fruit becomes heavy. A general rule for patio-type tomatoes is that minimum soil depth should be 8 inches. Unless you're using a half-barrel or something equally big, it's best to stay away from most heirlooms and beefsteak types, indeterminates with half-pound or bigger fruits.

In any case, the more growing space you can give the roots, the less watering and fertilizing you'll have to do and the less you'll need to worry about roots baking in the hot sun or chilling on a cool night. More soil means more insulation for the roots.

SOIL MIX

Ordinary garden soil isn't the best choice for use in pots. Compost can be used on its own in a large pot left outdoors, but soil alone won't work as well as it would if mixed with other materials that keep it from compacting into a solid lump that sheds water and slows root growth. A purchased potting-soil mixture will work well indoors or out. In fact, some gardeners who aren't fussy about appearance use the bag of potting soil itself, turned on one side, slit from end to end, then planted. If you want to make your own mixture, one recipe calls for equal parts topsoil, peat moss and sand. The peat moss can be replaced with leaf mold, bark fiber or coconut fiber. Rock wool, a substance made from basalt rock, is not easy to find unless you are a commercial grower, but it is a good additive that retains water and nutrients. For a lightweight container, replace the sand with vermiculite or perlite.

CONTAINER CHOICE

Almost anything can be used as a container, provided it is large enough, as described above, strong enough to hold wet soil for a season and stable enough that it won't tip over in the wind. The usual advice is that there be holes in the bottom of any container for excess water to drain out, but I have had better luck with a watertight container for a hanging basket or for any dry, windy place, such as a south-facing window box. As the plants grow, they use the water so quickly that it doesn't sit long in the bottom. Before winter, empty containers to avoid frost cracking.

HOUSEHOLD CONTAINERS: Many otherwise unlikely candidates, such as wicker baskets and cookie tins, become possibilities when they are lined with plastic.

TERRA-COTTA POTS: These, too, should be lined with plastic. Otherwise, they dry out too fast.

PLASTIC POTS: Generally, these are ideal —lightweight and watertight. Black plastic pots, the type that holds most purchased shrubs or trees, are suitable in every way but color. Experiments in Alabama showed that temperatures above about 113 degrees F—hot enough to kill root tips—could be reached in black plastic pots in the sun. In a cool place, this extra warming can be beneficial, but if your tomato will be growing in a hot place, especially in the south, use a light-colored container instead or enclose the black pot within a basket or wooden box.

BOXES: In a rooftop-garden demonstration in Montreal, described in Agriculture Canada's booklet "Container Gardening" (now out of print), all the vegetables were grown in wooden boxes, mostly recycled. The boxes averaged about 15 inches by 2 feet and 1 foot deep, large enough to grow two cherry-tomato plants. Along with the tomatoes, companion plants were sometimes included: basil, parsley or oregano. Basil, the booklet advises, should be planted as seeds, not seedlings, which "grow too quickly." About parsley, it says, "Use only the curly-leaved parsley, as the flat-leaf variety grows too quickly and too large." A purchased soil mix was used, the type that includes a lightweight ingredient such as perlite or vermiculite.

The Tomato Club newsletter (see Sources, page 88) of January/February 1995 includes detailed instructions for making boxes from squares of polystyrene foam. These boxes are meant for growing full-size tomatoes outdoors and are especially useful where the garden soil is contaminated with disease organisms or wherever there is a good sunny spot but not sufficient depth of soil for tomatoes. The advantage of the polystyrene foam (such as Styrofoam) is that it insulates the roots, keeping the temperature around them fairly constant. The foam, preferably about 2 inches thick, is cut into squares 22 inches on each side, nailed together at the corners, then bound around with plastic or steel twine for strength. The box is lined with plastic and filled with compost, then planted.

HALF-BARRELS: These can be purchased at many large garden shops and water-garden suppliers in spring. They are big enough to hold even a large-fruiting tomato. The soil can be reused from year to year, but remove and replace the top few inches to help control fungal diseases, and fertilize regularly. One grower reuses the barrel soil from year to year but fertilizes with every watering.

WATERING

Containers need frequent watering. The more root-bound the plant, the sunnier, warmer and windier the location and the more permeable the pot, the more watering will be required. Tomatoes need about 1 gallon of water per square foot of soil every week. That translates into a little more than a pint a day. But if the weather is hot and windy and the pot is small or terra-cotta, that pint can be gone in a few hours, leaving a wilting stem growing out of a block of dust. Mulching the soil will help, as will inserting cans, both ends removed, as Mimi Luebbermann did in the example cited earlier. Don't count on the rain to water your container plants. Chances are, plant foliage will shed almost every drop that falls on your little garden. If you have a lot of containers or are away frequently, you might want to invest in a drip-irrigation system.

Mixing hydrogels or absorbent polygels into the soil is sometimes recommended. These starch-based gels, available in garden stores, absorb hundreds of times their weight in water. Their effectiveness is controversial, however. For your own interest, try mixing hydrogels into one pot and leaving it out of another placed nearby, and compare the results.

Self-watering pots—both hanging and standing models— are available on the market. These pots include a reservoir at the bottom, where excess water is held for roots. You can create a similar effect in any pot that has a drainage hole by putting an inch or so of soil mix in the bottom of the pot, then setting into it a watertight container, such as a 1-pint dairy container or something else small enough to leave a ring of soil between the container and the pot wall and shallow enough that its rim doesn't stick out above the soil surface. This inner container will hold excess water, and the plant will extend some roots into this reservoir while other roots seek out the drier soil around the reservoir. A system like this is especially useful in a hanging basket, where evaporation is inevitably rapid.

PROTECTED CROPS

Container tomatoes are easiest to grow outdoors, because tomatoes like a lot of light, but if you have a bright enough spot indoors, you can also grow tomatoes under lights, in a south-facing window or in a home greenhouse. Johnny's Selected Seeds includes indoor containers within the umbrella term "protected crops," which describes plants grown under any type of cover, be they indoors or out. Protected crops can grow in the garden under rows of polyethylene, in cold frames, in freestanding greenhouses, in greenhouses attached to the house, on sunny windowsills or in basements under lights. As long as there are at least 6 hours of bright light every day and night temperatures under the cover are above about 60 de-

grees F, tomatoes will grow and set fruit. All of these protected plants also need special attention paid to watering, pests, diseases and pollination.

Johnny's points out that most fresh market tomatoes in Europe and Asia are grown not in open fields but in greenhouses or under polyethylene tunnels. "Even unheated poly tunnels can ripen tomatoes 3 to 4 weeks earlier than outdoors," says the catalog. These tunnels, described in Chapter 2, are made of transparent polyethylene held up on wire hoops. The soil under the tunnel is covered with a dark plastic mulch.

Protected plants like these have no extra heat except what they receive from the greenhouse effect. A transparent covering collects solar energy, extending the growing season by about a month at each end. In a greenhouse given supplementary heating, either from a source inside the greenhouse or from an attached building, growth can continue year-round, but there will be no fruiting from January to March unless there is supplementary light as well. Commercial growers use high-pressure sodium lamps, but these are so expensive to purchase and to use that any cost benefit of growing your own tomatoes would be lost.

HOME GREENHOUSES

The easiest way to grow greenhouse or indoor tomatoes is as a spring crop. Sow the seeds in late winter, a couple of months earlier than usual for outdoor growing. In the northern states and Canada, this means a mid-January start. The seedlings can be set into the growing beds as soon as the soil temperature remains above 55 degrees F day and night. The earlier this happens, the better the yields will be. As days lengthen, the plants respond by growing quickly, 67

Growing tomatoes in a greenhouse that is given no extra heat can extend the season by about 2 months, but adding heat allows year-round growth.

blossoming and setting fruit. Harvesting begins a month or two before outdoor tomatoes are ready and continues well into the beginning of the outdoor harvest. These greenhouse plants should bear heavily for 6 to 8 weeks.

For a fall crop, seeding should be done around early June. The seedlings are planted in early August and begin to bear in October. After this, they will probably not grow much or set new fruit, but the green fruit already on the vine will gradually ripen.

WINDOWSILL TOMATOES

While spring and fall are the easiest times to harvest fruit, requiring little or no extra lighting, small- or medium-fruited determinates can sometimes be coaxed to yield tomatoes in winter. Just don't expect these to have quite the fla-

vor or quality of their outdoor counterparts. Indoor plants must receive as much light as you can manage. A south-facing window is the minimal requirement for light. Supplementing that light with fluorescents will give the plants a boost. Burpee's suggests that seeds of 'Pixie' be sown in October for a February harvest or in January for an April harvest. Another way to have late fruit is to use cuttings of small-fruited outdoor plants. Dick Raymond, author of several best-selling gardening books, takes cuttings from his 'Pixie' plants toward the end of summer in Vermont. He removes the bottom leaves and puts the cuttings in jars of water to root. Then he plants them deeply in containers of purchased growing mix, two plants to a pot 10 inches wide. He keeps the soil constantly moist for a week to allow the roots to grow. When they bloom, he sprays the plants with Blossom Set, and Raymond says he has fresh tomatoes for Christmas salads.

GREENHOUSE VARIETY CHOICE

While commercial field tomatoes are generally determinates, commercial greenhouse growers almost always choose indeterminate varieties. These tall-growing vining tomatoes are trained on strings descending from the roof to make maximum use of the covered space and for easy picking. These indeterminates require well-controlled conditions, with bright light and supplementary heat. The large-fruited types need night temperatures around 72 degrees F or a bit higher. Some greenhouse hybrids are so highly developed that seed may cost close to $20 per packet.

While Johnny's, a seed company aimed at home gardeners, offers a good list of indeterminates, home gardeners can grow almost anything they choose in a greenhouse that is sufficiently warm and bright, provided the tomato doesn't require too much space. As described above, the smaller-fruited determinates are more forgiving than the indeterminates meant for the greenhouse. Whatever you choose, stay away from large-fruited indeterminates meant for the outdoor garden, especially types without inbred disease resistance. Here are a few of the varieties often recommended for greenhouses:

Boa VFFLT

This French greenhouse indeterminate, new in 1995, is recommended by Johnny's for protected crops in the east and for both outdoor and protected crops in the west. Stokes recommends 'Boa' for good flavor. The beefsteak-type fruit is similar in size to 'Buffalo' but earlier. The light green shoulders ripen red, and the fruit ripens from the inside out. The interior is light pink at the green, or blush, picking stage. 67 days.

Buffalo VFFT

This greenhouse indeterminate bears red, firm, 10-ounce fruit. "Considered by many to be the tastiest large-fruited variety," says Johnny's. 'Buffalo' is disease-resistant, and the tall vines are vigorous. 72 days.

Cobra VFT

This French hybrid has firm, 8-ounce, beefsteak-type fruit that ripens from the inside out. The Tomato Growers Supply Company says, "Excellent flavor causes many growers to consider this the best-tasting of the greenhouse-grown hybrids."

Greenhouse series

This hybrid series gives each tomato a number. New in 1996 was 'Greenhouse 761' VFFNTA, with smooth, red, 10-ounce fruit. "Tomatoes are big, attractive and offer fine flavor," says the Tomato Growers Supply Company catalog. First pick comes about 74 days from transplanting. 'Greenhouse 109' TV from Johnny's bears fruit that is generally larger than 'Buffalo,' maturing in about 77 days.

Hybrid Pink KR-381

Some gardeners prefer a pink tomato. This indeterminate from Stokes is a favorite in greenhouses in eastern Canada and Ohio, although it is sometimes grown outdoors. The fruit is extra-large, about half a pound. The vigorous vines must be staked.

Jumbo

An indeterminate with very high yields of extra-large red fruit, some over half a pound. 'Jumbo' does not have as much

69

PINCH OFF SHOOTS WHICH GROW IN THE JOINTS BETWEEN THE MAIN STEM AND THE LEAF STEMS

Greenhouse indeterminates yield more fruit if pruned to two main stems.

disease resistance as many others, but the larger fruit makes it appealing.

Sierra TF

"The earliest greenhouse variety of this midsize," says Johnny's Selected Seeds. Hybrid indeterminate vines yield glossy, bright red, tasty fruit weighing around 5 ounces in the early season, as heavy as 7 ounces in summer and early fall.

Tropic VFN

Developed by the University of Florida, this open-pollinated indeterminate can be grown indoors or out. It has good disease resistance and heavy yields of half-pound, firm red fruit. In greenhouses in Alberta, the fruit turned soft during June and July. It matures about 80 days after transplanting.

Vendor

One of the few open-pollinated green-house tomatoes still on the market (along with 'Tropic'), 'Vendor,' developed in Vineland, Ontario, is a favorite of home greenhouse growers for several reasons. Although it is an indeterminate, it has shorter vines, with fruit clusters closer together than most others, so it is easier to prune and pollinate. The firm red, 6-ounce fruit has good flavor. There is some disease resistance. "Excellent for outdoor staking and hydroponic growing," says Vesey's. Stokes recommends giving 'Vendor' more fertilizer than is needed by the hybrids.

GREENHOUSE PLANT CARE

Indeterminates in the greenhouse must be pruned if they are not to grow into an impenetrable tangle of vegetation. Although these tomatoes can be trained to just one stem, training to two stems increases the yield by at least one-third per plant. For two stems, only one early sucker (the shoot that grows in a leaf axil) below the first blossom cluster is allowed to grow, and all others are pinched out as soon as they appear. Pinching should be done at least twice a week. Lower leaves that yellow or fade should also be removed.

One common method of supporting the vines is by tying lengths of strong twine to a horizontal wire 6 to 8 feet above the soil surface. The bottom of one piece of twine is looped around the bottom of the main tomato stem, and another piece of twine is looped around the secondary stem. Both stems are wound around their own piece of twine as they grow. In home greenhouses, stakes can also be used. The support must be strong, because a full-grown vine loaded with fruit can weigh 25 pounds.

Pest control is a necessity in most greenhouses. In a confined space without natural predators, populations of pests can quickly get out of hand.

Tomatoes are adaptable to a simple homemade hydroponic system.

Whitefly is much more problematic inside than outdoors. Small outbreaks can be monitored or even controlled with bright yellow sticky cards suspended near the plants. Yellow cards will also catch fungus gnats and aphids on the wing. Larger outbreaks of whitefly can be checked with a beneficial insect predator, *Encarsia formosa*. Lady beetles can be introduced to a greenhouse for aphid control. Light blue sticky cards are favored for monitoring western flower thrips. Additional beneficial insects for control of most pests are available from some garden-supply companies. (See Sources, page 87.)

Most outdoor tomato flowers are self-pollinated by the wind—a mere breeze will do it—or by insects. In the greenhouse, however, you will generally have to pay some attention to pollination. This is an easy job, because as you brush past the plants in the greenhouse, you may inadvertently allow pollination to occur. Deliberately shaking the plants on bright days, preferably around noon, will do the job. Commercial greenhouses sometimes purchase bumblebees to pollinate tomatoes and peppers, or they may use a hand-held device called an electric bee, which vibrates entire trusses. If you'd rather use a spray, look for Blossom Set or Tomato Fruit Set.

Temperature is also important for pollination, which will not occur when the greenhouse is too cold or too hot. In experiments in North Carolina, the best night temperature for greenhouse tomato pollination was about 72 degrees F. Little or no fruit is set on most varieties below 50 degrees.

HYDROPONICS

Hydroponics is a method of growing plants without soil. Certain plants can't be grown this way, but tomatoes are quite amenable to the system. The roots are given some sort of substrate to grow through—anything from gravel to rock wool to a special polyurethane foam slab—and watered with a nutrient solution. The advantages can include less weight, fewer diseases and constant control of nutrients. The disadvantage is that plants are entirely dependent upon an almost constant drip of nutrient solution, so hydroponics can end up being the most labor- and energy-intensive way to grow tomatoes. Hydroponic systems are well suited to indoor or greenhouse tomatoes, but some systems can be used outdoors. Check the mail-order companies list in Sources for equipment and instructions.

71

From Fall to Winter

Taking Tomatoes From Garden to Kitchen

Chemistry may be able to explain the ripening of a tomato more accurately than poetry can, but there is nothing like that process to turn an ordinary gardener lyrical. A ripening tomato is simply a magical thing, the touch of nature's wand that rewards all that fussing and fretting in the tomato bed from spring through summer. As the weather warms, the green fruit swells and turns paler, takes on a whitish, then a pinkish blush, becomes orange, then red, softening and sweetening all the while.

Here is the chemistry: After pollination, tomato fruit needs 40 to 60 days of good weather to ripen. During the first 20 to 30 days of that stretch of time, the fruit gradually swells. Then, during the remaining time, the magic happens. The green chlorophyll gradually breaks down, so the fruit becomes whitish— a useful signal called "mature green," when fruit will continue ripening even if picked. During the next week, all the important things happen. The full color develops, acidity decreases, starch is converted into sugar, and essential oils and other precious components of flavor are created. Call the result the taste of sunshine, if you like. Tomatoes ripened indoors or in greenhouses never quite measure up.

How a tomato ripens depends partly upon variety. Varieties that have clear skin become pink or pale purple. Varieties with red flesh and yellow skin turn red. Temperature is important too. Lycopene, the red pigment, does not develop in fruits when the temperature is cooler than 50 degrees F or hotter than about 86 degrees, though in hot weather, the yellow pigments will continue to develop. Increasingly common are tomatoes with what is called the

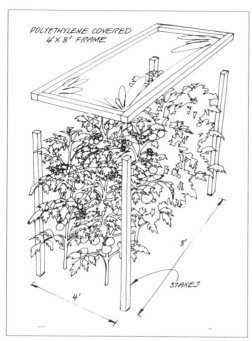

Covering garden plants may extend the tomato season more than 2 weeks.

uniform color gene. At the mature green stage, they are the same color all over, and they gradually turn uniformly red. Varieties such as 'Early Girl' and all the paste tomatoes ripen this way. Many other tomatoes, mostly home-garden types, have green shoulders that ripen later than the base of the fruit. This type is not favored by commercial growers because consumers want uniform color, but green shoulders sometimes signal better flavor.

Flavor depends to some extent upon variety, to some extent upon weather, soil and other influences. Some varieties are more acidic, some are sweeter. Acidity is independent of color and fairly consistent among varieties, but sugar content may be high or low, and the sweeter the tomato, the less you can taste the acid. So while you may think that a pink or white tomato is low in acid, chances are that it is simply higher in sugar. Rate of fertilization can also affect tomato flavor. Food scientists at Florida State University grew one type of tomato at three different rates of fertilization. The best tasting of the three, according to a panel of 16 people, were the tomatoes given the least fertilizer (2½ pounds of nitrogen and 4 pounds of potassium per 1,000 square feet).

EXTENDING THE SEASON

Harvesting becomes fast and frantic when fall days begin to cool, especially when a cold front has just passed and the weather forecasts threaten frost. Make no mistake—frost will damage your plants and any exposed fruit. An extended stretch of cold weather, even without frost, will also take its toll, but you may be able to coax an extra 2 weeks or more from the tomato season by sheltering the plants from the first frosts. Little growth or fruit setting will take place once nights have turned cool, but any protected fruit on the plants will ripen, and flavor will likely be better in fruit which ripens outdoors than in that brought indoors. Research by the United States Department of Agriculture (USDA) found that a key component of tomato flavor was 3 to 10 times as abundant in vine-ripened tomatoes as in tomatoes picked green and ripened off the vine.

If a frost is predicted, cover the plants with anything that is portable and light enough to avoid plant damage. Sheets, blankets, towels, tarps and plastic sheets can all be used. Weight down the edges or corners to keep the wind from blowing the covers off. If the cover will remain on the plants for more than a couple of days, it should be transparent, usually clear plastic. Covers that do not admit light should be removed during the day if the temperature has risen.

Entire plants can be pulled out and

Indoors, treat ripening tomatoes just as you would bananas. They keep best at a cool room temperature, not touching and out of direct sunlight.

hung upside down in a sheltered place for the fruit to continue ripening. Otherwise, as soon as the plants begin to die, you can clean out the tomato patch. Pick all fruit that is pale green or riper to continue ripening indoors. No, they won't be as good as those that ripened outdoors, but they will be just as good as anything in the supermarket, and the price will be right. Any fruit that has been touched by frost will not keep, nor will fruit that has suffered from chilling injury—exposure to a day or more under 40 degrees F even without frost. Fruit that is dark green and hard won't ripen either, but it can be picked for green-tomato relish and other preserves. Remove any cages or stakes and store them in a shed or garage, and pull out the plants. If they were diseased, burn the remains or pack them into garbage bags for the dump. Otherwise, pile them separately or put them through a shredder, because the stems left whole are too tough to add to the compost pile.

TOMATOES INDOORS

If you want tomatoes to ripen indoors, there will be less chance of spoilage if you first wash them in a solution of 1 part household bleach to 4 parts water. Rinse the fruit in tap water, then dry it. Whether mature green or ripe, tomatoes should be stored no cooler than 40 degrees F. Cooler temperatures cause deterioration in both flavor and texture. As one tomato marketer puts it, "Refrigeration murders tomato flavor. You should treat a tomato as though it were a banana. Let it ripen on the kitchen counter at room temperature." Mature green tomatoes are especially vulnerable to damage by chilling and do best at slightly warmer temperatures than those tolerated by ripe fruit. At 55 to 60 degrees, ripening takes place slowly, and most tomatoes will stay in good condition for 2 to 6 weeks. At 65 degrees, ripening occurs quickly, but tomatoes do not soften excessively. Above 70 degrees, ripening is rapid, and color, texture and flavor are adversely affected.

Best for storage is room temperature, 60 to 70 degrees F. Sunlight is not only unnecessary for storage or ripening but can be damaging. An easy way to store mature green fruit is in boxes between layers of paper towel or newspaper so that any fruit that does decay can be spotted and removed before the infection spreads. 'Long Keeper' tomatoes, described on page 48, should be picked before frost or before nights are consistently cooler than 50 degrees. Pick only the fruit that is ripe or changing from green to yellowish orange at the blossom end. The fruit can be spread out in a single layer, not touching, on a kitchen shelf or any protected place at room temperature and away from direct sunlight. Only perfect, unbruised and unblemished fruit should be stored this way. 'Long Keeper' is ready to eat when the skin is golden orange.

When it comes time to use your tomatoes, don't slice them and leave them sitting around. They taste best if eaten soon after slicing, which releases volatile flavor constituents. California agricultural chemist Ronald G. Buttery says, "That's why the tomato you put in your sandwich when you're packing your lunch in the morning doesn't really have that much fresh tomato flavor by noon."

SAVING SEEDS

Open-pollinated, or nonhybrid, tomatoes are the best type to grow if you want to save your own seed. These seeds will probably grow into a plant much like the parent, especially if there was not another variety growing within 10 feet. Currant tomatoes are especially likely to cross with other types, so they should be grown in a separate part of the garden, at least 25 feet away from other tomatoes. Save seeds only from the healthiest plants that exhibit qualities you want. If possible, allow the fruit to become overripe before you pick it for seed. To save the seeds, simply cut open an unwashed, fully mature tomato and squeeze the pulp and seeds into a jar. Discard the empty tomato shell. If you are using greenhouse, hydroponic or indoor fruit, add a pinch of garden soil to the jar to supply the needed microorganisms that are naturally present on the skin of outdoor fruits. The liquid needs to ferment. Allow the jar of pulp and seeds to stand at room temperature for a couple of days. Then pour the mixture into a sieve, run tap water over it till the seeds are clean, spread the cleaned seeds on a paper towel, and allow them to dry thoroughly. Wet seeds will germinate. Store the seeds in labeled envelopes kept in closed jars or tins in a cool, dark place. Tomato seeds should remain viable for several years.

DRYING

Sun-dried tomatoes are expensive gourmet treats that can be duplicated fairly easily at home. The surest way to dry tomatoes properly is in a dehydrator, but this investment is worthwhile only if you intend to dry more than a few. If you live in a hot, dry climate, drying can be done outdoors, the traditional way. The variety 'Principe Borghese,' listed on page 44, is grown in Italy specifically for drying outdoors. Renee Shepherd of Shepherd's Garden Seeds

Home-dried tomatoes can be stored as is or in olive oil with herbs.

says, "In Sicily at harvesttime, farm-houses are decorated with long bunches of these red little rounded, egg-shaped beauties, drying in the sun. We halve and dry them in large quantities, then put them up—some plain, some in olive oil with fresh rosemary or thyme."

But any tomato can be dried. It just has to stay warm enough and dry fast enough to prevent mold from growing. The drier the tomato is to begin with or the smaller it is or the more thinly sliced it is, the faster it will dry, whatever the variety. Ethel Brennan and Georgeanne Brennan, co-authors of *Sun-Dried Tomatoes* (see Sources, page 88) are especially fond of the flavor of 'Evergreen, 'Green Grape' and 'Early Girl.'

There should be air circulation both over and under the tomatoes; outdoors, a bamboo vegetable steamer tray works well, as does a wooden frame over which plastic window screen or muslin has been stretched. Stay away from galvanized, fiberglass, vinyl or copper screen. In my somewhat cool climate, I have been able to partially sun-dry tomatoes on a warm summer day, but then moved them into my gas oven to finish. The heat from the pilot light is not quite adequate to dry tomatoes without their starting to mold, so I heat the oven to 150 degrees F, turn the oven off, then put in the tomatoes on their racks and let them sit in the oven for a day or so, till they are leathery and pliable and a handful will not stick together. Prolonged temperatures over about 140 degrees will cook the tomatoes rather than just dry them. Let them cool before storing them. If there is any mold at all, throw them out. Pack the sound ones into plastic bags, then, for safest storage, freeze them. Otherwise they can be packed in sterilized jars, covered in top-quality olive oil and kept in the refrigerator. If you opt for this last method, you can use not only the tomatoes in cooking but also the oil.

FREEZING

If drying tomatoes is the cheapest way to keep them into winter, then the easiest way is to freeze them whole. Keep only perfect fruits, or cut off any damaged parts, wash them and pack them into freezer bags. When you remove them from the bags, put them in cold water for about a minute, and the skins will peel off easily. You can also freeze stewed tomatoes or any sauces or condiments, but if you use rigid containers, such as dairy containers or glass jars, leave about one-quarter of the space empty at the top, because these liquids will expand as they freeze and can break a container. Frozen tomatoes can be cooked in any recipe calling for fresh ones, or they can be used to make sauces and condiments.

PEELING

To peel fresh tomatoes, blanch them by dipping them in boiling water for 30 to 60 seconds—the duration depends on ripeness, size and variety—then dipping them briefly in cold water before removing the skin.

CANNING

At one time, the process called canning used metal cans. Now glass jars with metal lids and screw tops are the easiest and safest method. The advantage with canned tomatoes is that they can be stored safely for a long time at room temperature, though they are best kept in a cool, dark place to prevent discoloration. Follow recipes, timings and procedures exactly to prevent off flavors or the development of toxins within the jars. Don't use cracked or chipped jars. If the food inside the jar looks or smells suspicious, discard it without tasting it. Also if, after storage, you find that some tops are not sealed, discard the food. Properly sealed lids cannot be lifted easily with your fingers.

Quantities
• 1 bushel (53 pounds) of tomatoes makes 17 to 20 quarts of canned tomatoes.
• 1 quart of canned tomatoes requires 2½ to 3 pounds of tomatoes.
• 8 pounds of paste tomatoes cook down to about 3 cups of sauce.

Sterilizing Jars
Sterilize jars and lids, new or used, by one of the following methods, according to Agriculture Canada's booklet, *Pickles and Relishes:*

| | |

The Vertues of Love Apples

In the hot Countries where they naturally growe, they are much eaten of the people, to coole and quench the heate and thirst of their hot stomaches. The Apples also boyled, or infused in oyle in the sunne, is thought to be good to cure the itch, assuredly it will allay the heate thereof.
—*John Parkinson,* Paradisi in Sole, Paradisus Terrestris, *London, 1629.*

OVEN: Wash jars and lids in hot, soapy water. Rinse well. Preheat oven to 250 degrees F. Set jars and lids on the oven rack. Heat 10 minutes. Remove from oven as needed.

BOILING WATER: Wash in warm, soapy water. Rinse well. Invert jars in 2 inches of water. Bring water to a boil and let boil 15 minutes. Leave the jars in the hot water till needed.

DISHWASHER: Jars and lids can be washed, rinsed and sterilized in the dishwasher. Make sure the cycle is set at the highest water temperature.

Basic Canning Recipes
The following are based on those in Agriculture Canada's booklet *Canning Canadian Fruits and Vegetables.*

QUARTERED TOMATOES:
1) Choose only ripe, high-quality fruit.
2) Peel, as above. Remove cores and any green or damaged areas.
3) Sterilize lids and jars as described above.
4) Cut tomatoes in quarters. Place in pot and heat to boiling, stirring to prevent sticking and adding water only if necessary.

5) Pack hot in jars, leaving head space. Add ½ teaspoon pickling or kosher salt to each pint jar, 1 teaspoon to each quart jar, then follow directions for "Filling Jars."

6) Process pint jars in boiling water for 35 minutes, 1-quart jars for 45 minutes.

WHOLE TOMATOES: Follow the directions for quartered tomatoes, above, but leave whole. Pack raw tomatoes in jars, then cover with boiling tomato juice. Process pint jars for 40 minutes, 1-quart jars for 50 minutes.

TOMATO JUICE:

1) Select only ripe, firm, juicy tomatoes. Do not use soft-ripe, heavily bruised or severely cracked fruit.

2) Wash fruit, and trim out any small bruised or decayed spots.

3) Prepare lids, jars and boiling-water bath.

4) Cut tomatoes in quarters. With a potato masher, crush some of these in the bottom of a large pot, heating to boiling while stirring and crushing. Continue to add quarters at a rate slow enough to keep the mixture simmering. Continue crushing and stirring.

5) Remove from heat 5 minutes after the last tomatoes have been added.

6) Put through a tomato mill, or press through a sieve. Reheat to boiling.

7) Fill jars, as described below.

8) Process either size of jar for 35 minutes.

9) Juice may settle in storage. Shake before using.

Filling Jars

Place the hot, sterilized jars, not touching, on a folded dish towel. Pack in tomatoes loosely enough to allow liquid to fill in all around them. For liquids, there are funnels available that will fit standard canning jars. Fill the jars to within ½ inch of the rim. To be sure that acidity is high enough for safe storage, add ¼ teaspoon citric acid or 1 tablespoon reconstituted lemon juice to pint jars, and double that amount for quart jars. Citric acid crystals can be purchased in most pharmacies. If necessary, remove air bubbles by running a knife blade down the inside of the jar. Wipe the rim of the jar with a clean, damp cloth before setting on the lid.

Place the metal lid on the jar, and tighten the screw band.

Processing

Process jars in a boiling-water bath deep enough to cover the lids with at least 2 inches of water. Fill the bath about half full, and heat the water until it is about the same temperature as the filled jars, then set the jars in the basket and lower them into the hot water. Top with more hot water, if necessary. Bring to a boil, and begin timing when the water boils again.

When the time is up, turn off the heat and open the lid away from you. Using oven mitts, lift the basket out of the hot water. There are special jar lifters for removing the hot jars, or you can use oven mitts. Place the hot jars, not touching, on a folded towel to cool. Metal snap lids make a snapping sound as they contract and seal. When sealed, they are slightly concave. Do not move the jars until they are cool. Label with date and contents before storing.

Storage

Canned goods are best kept in a cool, dark, dry place. Light can change the color of the preserve, and too warm a spot can cause the flavor to deteriorate. After jars are opened, they should be stored in the refrigerator. For full development of flavor, uncooked pickles should be stored 4 to 6 weeks before they are opened. Cooked products such as juices, chutneys and jams can be eaten right away.

If there is any sign of spoilage, discard the food without tasting it.

NUTRIENTS

Tomatoes are a good dietary source of vitamins C and A, mostly because they are consumed in such large amounts. In a survey conducted at the University of California at Davis, tomatoes ranked just 13th among popular fruits and vegetables in vitamin C content, and 16th in vitamin A content. However, they took first place as a source of both these nutrients in the American diet because they are consumed in far greater quantity than more nutritious vegetables such as broccoli. According to *Tomatoes: Fruit and Vegetable Facts and Pointers,* published in Washington D.C. in 1969, 3.5 ounces (100 grams) of raw tomato contains: 93 grams of water, 22 calories, 1.1 grams of protein, 0.2 gram of fat, 4.7 grams of carbohydrate, .5 gram of fiber, 0.5 gram of ash, 13 mg of calcium, 27 mg of phosphorus, 14 mg of magnesium, 900 International Units of vitamin A and 13 to 20 mg of vitamin C (ascorbic acid). Certain varieties of tomatoes have much more vitamin A or vitamin C. For high vitamin A, grow 'Carorich' or another of the orange varieties. For high vitamin C, look to currant tomatoes and cherry tomatoes, some of which contain 45 to 50 mg per 100 grams, two to five times the content of most other varieties. Tomatoes retain their ascorbic acid content well. After 3 weeks at room temperature, there is little appreciable loss. Even ketchup is modestly nutritious. It's a good thing because, according to Andrew F. Smith, author of *Pure Ketchup: A History of America's National Condiment with Recipes* (University of South Carolina Press, 1996), ketchup bottles are found in 97 percent of American households, and 80 percent of American restaurants have easily accessible bottles. Americans consume about three bottles per person every year.

RECIPES

Salsa Cruda

Salsa simply means sauce, but here it refers to the raw tomato chutney at the center of every Mexican table, eaten as a dip for tortilla chips or as a side dish. The key to an authentic salsa is fresh cilantro. Cooks often substitute parsley, but only cilantro lures the flavor of Mexico into a northern kitchen. Add the jalapeño last, stirring in half a teaspoon at a time until it is hot enough for you.

4	fresh ripe tomatoes
1	green bell pepper
1	medium Spanish onion
1	large clove garlic, minced
1	fresh jalapeño pepper *or*

Salsa cruda is a fresh sauce essential to authentic Mexican cuisine.

1 Tbsp. canned hot pepper, seeded and finely chopped
2 Tbsp. minced fresh coriander leaves
1 Tbsp. extra-virgin olive oil
Juice of 1 lime
Salt & pepper

Seed the tomatoes (see below) and chop finely. Mix together all the ingredients, and marinate for 2 to 6 hours.

Adjust the seasonings to your taste, adding more garlic and jalapeño if you like a salsa that is lip-scorching hot. Drain the salsa to serve, but keep it marinating in its liquid in the refrigerator, where it keeps for 2 days without losing quality.

Makes 2 cups.

SEEDING TOMATOES: Before chopping a tomato for salad, seed it by cutting it in half crosswise and squeezing gently, prying the gel and seeds out of the cavities. Some thick-skinned tomatoes need to be peeled. With a sharp knife, cut a light X on the bottom of the fruit, then drop it into simmering water for a few seconds, until the skin at the X curls. Plunge immediately into cold water. When cool, the skin slips off easily.

Insalata Caprese
This delicious salad is a standard summer first course in sunny Italy.

Whole basil leaves
2 fresh ripe tomatoes, sliced
½ lb. fresh mozzarella cheese (Bocconcini), sliced thickly
¼ cup extra-virgin olive oil
2 Tbsp. red-wine vinegar
½ tsp. balsamic vinegar
1 Tbsp. finely chopped basil leaves
Freshly ground black pepper

Arrange whole basil leaves on a platter. 81

Fan tomato slices on the basil, alternating with slices of mozzarella. Beat the oil, vinegars and chopped basil until emulsified. Pour over the tomato and mozzarella slices, and top with a generous grinding of pepper. For a variation, omit the cheese and sprinkle with 2 tablespoons of roasted pine nuts.

For a warm winter salad, omit the whole basil leaves, dress the tomato slices, then lay the cheese on top. Slide under the broiler until the cheese bubbles gently, then remove from oven, garnish with fresh parsley, and serve.

Serves 4.

Herbed Cherry Tomatoes

12-15	cherry tomatoes
4 Tbsp.	sunflower seed oil
2 tsp.	vinegar
1 tsp.	sugar
1 tsp.	oregano leaves *or* ½ tsp. powdered
1 tsp.	salt
½ tsp.	pepper
¼ tsp.	sweet basil

Slice tomatoes in half and put in a serving bowl. Combine remaining ingredients and pour over the tomatoes.

Cover and refrigerate for at least 2 hours before serving.

Serves 6.

Dilled Tomato Soup

This soup can also be made with canned or frozen tomatoes. The dill, however, must be fresh—this is what gives the soup its delicious, definitive flavor.

10	large ripe tomatoes
1	large onion
2	cloves garlic, minced
3 Tbsp.	butter
5 Tbsp.	flour
2 tsp.	tomato paste

5 cups	chicken stock
1 cup	whipping cream
4 Tbsp.	dill weed
	Salt & pepper

Coarsely chop 8 tomatoes. Chop onion and sauté in butter with garlic and half of the chopped tomatoes for 3 minutes. Remove from heat. Blend in flour, tomato paste and stock and bring to a boil. Lower heat, add remaining chopped tomatoes and simmer for 15 minutes. Add cream.

Peel and chop remaining 2 tomatoes and add to soup with dill, salt and pepper. Heat through, stirring well so that the cream does not curdle.

Serves 8.

Chicken With Tomatoes & Cream

When made with homegrown tomatoes and basil, this is especially good as a light summer supper. Home-frozen tomatoes and basil (just wash basil, dry thoroughly, chop and freeze in plastic bags) will also result in a fresh summery taste in midwinter.

2	whole chicken breasts, halved
3 Tbsp.	butter
1	clove garlic, minced
1	small onion, minced
3 Tbsp.	flour
¼ cup	white wine
1 cup	chopped tomatoes
½ cup	light cream
¼ cup	chopped fresh basil & parsley, mixed
	Salt & pepper

Place chicken breasts in a saucepan with enough salted water to cover, and poach until tender—about 20 minutes. Remove, reserving stock. Skin and bone chicken and set aside. In a large pan, melt butter and sauté garlic and onion. Add flour and stir well. Whisk in wine and ½ cup stock, and cook over high heat until sauce is reduced, stirring constantly. Reduce heat to medium, add tomatoes, cream and basil-parsley mixture, and cook for 4 to 5 minutes. Fold in chicken. Add salt and pepper to taste. Serve on toast, over rice or in pita pockets.

Serves 4.

Black Bean & Tomato Salad

1 cup	cooked black turtle beans
1 Tbsp.	cider vinegar or lemon juice
2 Tbsp.	olive oil
	Salt & pepper
1	large onion, chopped
2	large ripe tomatoes, chopped, *or* 1½ cups cherry tomatoes
2	cloves garlic, chopped

While beans are still warm, place in a large bowl and mix with vinegar or lemon juice, oil and salt and pepper to taste. Chill, then add onion, tomatoes and garlic, combining well. Chill overnight.

Serves 4.

Tomato Cheese Pie

FILLING
2 Tbsp.	butter
¼ cup	chopped green onions
1 cup	bread crumbs
¼ cup	chopped parsley
1 tsp.	basil
⅛ tsp.	salt
	Freshly ground black pepper
10	firm ripe tomatoes, peeled

TOPPING
1 cup	flour
1½ tsp.	baking powder
½ tsp.	salt
2 Tbsp.	butter
¼ cup	milk
½ cup	grated Cheddar cheese

Melt butter in a skillet. Add onions and cook for 3 to 4 minutes. Stir in bread crumbs and cook until golden. Remove from heat; stir in parsley, basil, salt and pepper to taste.

Cut tomatoes into ½-inch-thick slices. Place half the slices in a greased pie plate. Sprinkle with half the bread-crumb mixture. Repeat.

Sift together flour, baking powder and salt. Cut in butter to make fine crumbs. Add milk to make a soft dough, then work in cheese. Knead until smooth, wrap and refrigerate for 1 hour. On a lightly floured surface, roll dough to a 9-by-12-inch rectangle, ½ inch thick. Cut into 12 strips ½ inch wide. Make lattice top for pie, crimping edges to pan. Bake at 350 degrees F for 30 to 35 minutes, until crust is golden.

Serves 6 to 8.

Fresh Tomato & Cabbage Soup

2 Tbsp.	butter
1	clove garlic, crushed
2 cups	coarsely chopped cabbage
1 tsp.	salt
2 Tbsp.	flour
4	fresh ripe tomatoes, peeled, seeded & chopped
2 Tbsp.	parsley
½ tsp.	basil
⅛ tsp.	celery seed
⅛ tsp.	pepper
2 cups	milk

Melt butter, and sauté garlic and cabbage for 3 to 4 minutes. Add 2 cups water and salt, bring to a boil, reduce heat and simmer for 5 minutes. Dissolve flour in ¼ cup water, then stir into soup, cooking until thickened. Add tomatoes, parsley, basil, celery seed and pepper. Simmer for 5 to 10 minutes, stirring often. Stir in milk and heat through.

Serves 4 to 6.

Sources

SEEDS & PLANTS

ALBERTA NURSERIES & SEEDS LTD.
P.O. Box 20
Bowden, AB T0M 0K0
Phone 403-224-3544
Fax 403-224-2455
Catalog free to Canada; $2 to U.S.

BOUNTIFUL GARDENS
Ecology Action
5798 Ridgewood Road
Willits, CA 95490
Phone 707-459-6410
All seeds nonhybrid. Catalog free
to U.S.; $2 (U.S.) to Canada.

THE COOK'S GARDEN
P.O. Box 535
Londonderry, VT 05148-0535
Phone 802-824-3400; fax 802-824-3027
Catalog free.

DeGIORGI SEED CO.
6011 'N' Street
Omaha, NE 68117-1634
Phone 402-731-3901
Fax 402-731-8475
Organically grown seeds.
Catalog $2.

DOMINION SEED HOUSE
P.O. Box 2500
Georgetown, ON L7G 5L6
Phone 905-873-3037
Fax 800-282-5746
Catalog free, to Canada only.

ED HUME SEEDS
P.O. Box 1450
Kent, WA 98032
Phone 206-859-1110
Fax 206-859-0694
Seeds. Catalog $1 to the U.S.,
$2 to Canada.

FERRY-MORSE SEEDS
P.O. Box 488
Fulton, KY 42041-0488
Phone 800-626-3392 or 502-472-3400
Fax 502-472-3402
Catalog free.

GLECKLER'S SEEDMEN
Metamora, OH 43540
Phone 419-923-5463
Catalog free to the U.S.; $1 to Canada.

HARRIS SEEDS
60 Saginaw Drive, P.O. Box 22960
Rochester, NY 14692-2960
Phone 716-442-0100
Fax 713-442-9386
Catalog free, U.S. only.

HEIRLOOM SEEDS
P.O. Box 245
West Elizabeth, PA 15088-0245
Catalog $1, refundable with order.

JOHNNY'S SELECTED SEEDS
Foss Hill Road
Albion, Maine 04901
Phone 207-437-9294
Fax 207-437-2165
Catalog free.

J.W. JUNG SEED CO.
335 S. High Street
Randolph, WI 53957-0001
Phone 800-297-3123
Fax 800-692-5864
Catalog free, U.S. only.

LIBERTY SEED COMPANY
P.O. Box 806
New Philadelphia, OH 44663-0806
Phone 800-541-6022 or 330-364-1611
Fax 330-364-6415
Catalog free, U.S. only.

LOCKHART SEEDS, INC.
P.O. Box 1361

Stockton, CA 95205
Phone 209-466-4401
Fax 209-466-9766
Orders must be over $10.
U.S. only.

McFAYDEN SEED CO. LTD.
30 9th Street
Suite 200
Brandon, MB R7A 6N4
Phone 204-725-7300
Fax 204-725-1888
Catalog free.

OTIS S. TWILLEY SEED CO.
P.O. Box 65
Trevose, PA 19053-9467
Phone 215-639-8800 or 800-622-7333
Catalog free.

PARK SEED COMPANY
1 Parkton Avenue
Greenwood, SC 29647-0001
Phone 864-223-7333
Fax 864-941-4206
Catalog free.

SEED SAVERS EXCHANGE
3076 North Winn Road
Decorah, IA 52101
A nationwide volunteer seed exchange
dedicated to preserving heirloom and
other nonhybrid vegetables. For
information, send $1 (U.S.).

SEEDS BLÜM
HC 33 Idaho City Stage
Boise, ID 83706
Phone 800-742-1423 or 208-342-0858
Fax 208-338-5658

SEEDS OF CHANGE
P.O. Box 15700
Santa Fe, NM 87506-5700
Phone 505-438-8080
Fax 505-438-7052
Catalog free.

SEEDS OF DIVERSITY CANADA
P.O. Box 36, Station Q
Toronto, ON M4T 2L7
Phone 905-623-0353
Nonhybrid and heirloom seed
exchange. Membership $25.

SEEDS TRUST: HIGH ALTITUDE GARDENS
P.O. Box 1048
Hailey, ID 83333
Phone 208-788-4363
Fax 208-788-3452
All seeds nonhybrid. Catalog free.

SHEPHERD'S GARDEN SEEDS
30 Irene Street
Torrington, CT 06790-6658
Phone 860-482-3638
Fax 860-482-0532
or
6119 Highway 9
Felton, CA 95018
Phone 408-335-6910
Fax 408-335-2080
Catalog free.

SOUTHERN EXPOSURE SEED EXCHANGE
P.O. Box 170
Earlysville, VA 22936
Phone 804-973-4703
Fax 804-973-8717
Catalog $2, refundable with order.

STOKES SEEDS INC.
P.O. Box 548
Buffalo, NY 14240-0548
Phone 716-695-6980
Fax 716-695-9649
or
39 James Street, P.O. Box 10
St. Catharines, ON L2R 6R6
Phone 905-688-4300
Fax 905-684-8411
Catalog free.

T&T SEEDS LTD.
P.O. Box 1710

Winnipeg, MB R3C 3P6
Phone 204-956-2777
Fax 204-956-1994
Catalog free.

TERRITORIAL SEED COMPANY
P.O. Box 157
Cottage Grove, OR 97424
Phone 541-942-9547
Fax 541-942-9881
or
TERRITORIAL SEEDS CANADA LTD.
P.O. Box 750
206 - 8475 Ontario Street
Vancouver, BC V5X 3E8
Phone 604-482-8800
Fax 604-482-8822
Catalog free.

THOMPSON & MORGAN, INC.
P.O. Box 1308
Jackson, NJ 08527-0308
Phone 800-274-7333
Fax 908-363-9356
Catalog free.

TOMATO GROWERS SUPPLY COMPANY
P.O. Box 2237
Fort Myers, FL 33902
Phone 941-768-1119
Fax 941-768-3476
Seeds. More than 200 cultivars as well
as supplies and books.

VESEY'S SEEDS LTD.
York, PEI C0A 1P0
Phone 902-368-7333
Fax 902-566-1620
Catalog free.

W. ATLEE BURPEE CO.
300 Park Avenue
Warminster, PA 18974
Phone orders 800-888-1447
Customer service 800-333-5808
Fax 800-487-5530
Catalog free, to U.S. only.

WILLIAM DAM SEEDS
P.O. Box 8400
Dundas, ON L9H 6M1
Phone 905-628-6641
Fax 905-627-1729
Catalog $2.

EQUIPMENT & SUPPLIES

BETTER YIELD INSECTS CANADA
1302 Highway 2, RR3
Belle River, ON, Canada N0R 1A0
Phone 519-727-6108 (or in Canada,
    800-662-6562)
Fax 519-727-5989
Beneficial insects and organic pest
control. Catalog free.

BUMPER-CROP
1316 Centre Street North
Calgary, AB, Canada T2E 2R7
Phone 403-276-1345 (or in Canada,
    800-661-1228)
Fax 403-276-9120
Hydroponic supplies and information;
beneficial insects. Catalog $2.

CHARLEY'S GREENHOUSE SUPPLY
1569 Memorial Highway
Mount Vernon, WA 98273-9721
Phone 800-322-4707
Fax 800-233-3078

GARDENER'S SUPPLY COMPANY
128 Intervale Road
Burlington, VT 05401
Phone 800-315-4005 (U.S. only)
Irrigation equipment, greenhouses,
to U.S. only. Catalog free.

GEMPLER'S
P.O. Box 270
211 Blue Mounds Road
Mt. Horeb, WI 53572-0270
Phone 800-272-7672 or 800-551-1128
Greenhouse, pest control and
watering supplies.

GREENTREES
2464 S. Santa Fe Avenue
Vista, CA 92084
Phone 800-772-1997
    or 619-598-7551
Fax 619-598-6486
Hydroponic systems.
Catalog free.

HOME CANNING SUPPLY & SPECIALTIES
2017 La Brea Street
P.O. Box 1158
Ramona, CA 92065
Phone 619-788-0520
Fax 619-789-4745
All supplies needed for home canning.
Catalog free.

LEE VALLEY TOOLS LTD.
P.O. Box 6295, Station J
Ottawa, ON K2A 1T4
Phone 800-267-8767
Fax 800-668-1807
or
12 East River Street
Ogdensburg, NY 13669
Phone 800-871-8158
Fax 800-513-7885
Self-watering pots, light stands,
mulches, fabric covers, Wall-O-Water.
Catalog free.

THE NATURAL GARDENING COMPANY
217 San Anselmo Avenue
San Anselmo, CA 94960
Phone 707-766-9303
Fax 707-766-9747
Tomato spirals, greenhouses, irrigation
supplies, pest control, mulches, Wall-
O-Water. Catalog free.

PEACEFUL VALLEY FARM SUPPLY
P.O. Box 2209
Grass Valley, CA 95945
Phone 916-272-4769
Fax 916-272-4794
Catalog free.

SEASON EXTENDERS
P.O. Box 312
Stratford, CT 06497
Greenhouse and indoor garden
supplies. Catalog free.

INFORMATION

THE TOMATO CLUB
114 E. Main Street
Bogota, NJ 07603
Phone 201-488-2231
Fax 201-489-4609
Six issues a year for $15.95 to the U.S.;
$18.95 (U.S.) to Canada.

SUN-DRIED TOMATOES
Ethel Brennan and Georgeanne
  Brennan
Chronicle Books
275 Fifth Street
San Francisco, CA 94103

Index

Credits

Photographs

TURID FORSYTH: Pages 4, 6, 9, 10, 12, 21, 24, 26, 37, 39, 42, 47, 48, 49, 50, 56, 57, 58, 59, 72, 75, 77, 81

WALTER CHANDOHA: Pages 15, 27, 28, 29, 30 (left and right), 31, 32, 33, 36, 41, 44, 45, 62, 64

STEPHEN ERRINGTON: Page 68

Illustrations

IAN GRAINGE: Pages 16, 18, 20, 70, 71, 74